First World War
and Army of Occupation
War Diary
France, Belgium and Germany

25 DIVISION
7 Infantry Brigade,
Brigade Machine Gun Company
12 January 1916 - 28 February 1918

WO95/2244/6

The Naval & Military Press Ltd
www.nmarchive.com
Published in association with The National Archives

Published by

The Naval & Military Press Ltd

Unit 10 Ridgewood Industrial Park,

Uckfield, East Sussex,

TN22 5QE England

Tel: +44 (0) 1825 749494

www.naval-military-press.com

www.nmarchive.com

This diary has been reprinted in facsimile from the original. Any imperfections are inevitably reproduced and the quality may fall short of modern type and cartographic standards.

© Crown Copyright
Images reproduced by permission of The National Archives, London, England, 2015.

Contents

Document type	Place/Title	Date From	Date To
Heading	WO95/2244-6		
Heading	7th Machine Gun Coy. Jan 1916-Feb 1918		
Heading	7th Bde. Machine Gun Coy., January, 1916		
Heading	7th Bde Machine Gun Co. Jan Vol I		
War Diary	Ploegsteert	12/01/1916	22/01/1916
War Diary	La Becque	23/01/1916	25/01/1916
War Diary	Min to Vapeur Sheet 27 X 24.c.0.1	26/01/1916	30/01/1916
Heading	7th Bde. Machine Gun Coy. February 1916		
War Diary	Bailleul	31/01/1916	28/02/1916
Heading	7th Bde. Machine Gun Coy. March 1916		
Heading	10th Battn Cheshire Regiment October 1916		
Heading	7 Bde M.G. Coy. Vol III		
War Diary	Bailleul	29/02/1916	10/03/1916
War Diary	Robecq	11/03/1916	11/03/1916
War Diary	Brias	12/03/1916	16/03/1916
War Diary	Penin	17/03/1916	31/03/1916
Heading	7th Bde. Machine Gun Coy. April 1916		
War Diary	Field	01/04/1916	28/04/1916
Miscellaneous	D.A.G. 3rd Echelon BEF	30/04/1916	30/04/1916
Heading	7th Bde. Machine Gun Coy., May. 1916		
War Diary	Mt. St. Eloy.	01/05/1916	31/05/1916
Miscellaneous	7th Bde M.G. Coy.		
Heading	7th Bde. Machine Gun Coy. June 1916		
War Diary	Mt St Eloy	01/06/1916	02/06/1916
War Diary	Herlin Le Vert	03/06/1916	03/06/1916
War Diary	G. 2.1.7 Rf Lens Sheet No. 11	05/06/1916	12/06/1916
War Diary	Averdoingt F2.31	13/06/1916	13/06/1916
War Diary	Beauvois Lend Sheet 1/10,000 D4,4.8	14/06/1916	16/06/1916
War Diary	Longuevillete (D5, 36)	17/06/1916	17/06/1916
War Diary	Halloy Les Pernois (C6, 46)	18/06/1916	25/06/1916
War Diary	Halloy-Lez Pernois	26/06/1916	27/06/1916
War Diary	Puchevillers	28/06/1916	30/06/1916
Heading	7th Machine Gun Company. July 1916		
War Diary	Somme	30/06/1916	29/07/1916
Miscellaneous	7th Bde. M.G. Coy.		
Heading	7th Brigade. Machine Gun Company August 1916		
War Diary	Somme	01/08/1916	29/08/1916
Heading	7th. Machine Gun Company September 1916		
War Diary	In the Field	30/08/1916	15/09/1916
War Diary	Ribeaucourt	16/09/1916	24/09/1916
War Diary	Gezaincourt	25/09/1916	25/09/1916
War Diary	Arqueves	26/09/1916	28/09/1916
War Diary	Hedauville	29/09/1916	30/09/1916
Heading	7th Bde. Machine Gun Coy. October 1916		
War Diary	X2a Central	30/09/1916	14/10/1916
War Diary	W 89. Central	15/10/1916	21/10/1916
War Diary	Bouzincourt	22/10/1916	22/10/1916
War Diary	Herissart	23/10/1916	23/10/1916
War Diary	Gezaincourt	24/10/1918	24/10/1918
War Diary	Candas	25/10/1918	30/10/1918

Heading	7th Bde. Machine Gun Coy., November 1916		
War Diary	Le Bizet	31/10/1916	28/11/1916
Heading	7th Bde. Machine Gun Coy., December 1916		
War Diary	Le Bizet	29/11/1916	17/01/1917
War Diary	Carters Camp	18/01/1917	26/01/1917
Heading	70th Inf Bde	27/02/1917	27/02/1917
War Diary	Camp T 26.d.4.2. Res. Map 28 S.W. 1/10.000	27/01/1916	30/01/1916
War Diary	Ploegsteert Sector	02/02/1917	17/02/1917
War Diary	Ref Trench Map 28. S.W. 4 1/10000		
War Diary	Ploegsteert Sector	18/02/1917	22/02/1917
War Diary	Camp T26.d 4.2 Ref Map 28. S.W. 1/10.000	23/02/1917	23/02/1917
War Diary	Plebrouck	24/02/1917	11/03/1917
War Diary	Sheet 36A 1/40.000 Wellon Capell C4 B 0.6	12/03/1917	20/03/1917
War Diary	Sheet 36 A.1 in 40.000 Borre	20/03/1917	21/03/1917
War Diary	Bleu	22/03/1917	23/03/1917
War Diary	Sheet 28 1:40.000 Fme Du Bois		
War Diary	Sheet 36 NW 1:20.000	24/03/1917	24/03/1917
War Diary	Blanche Maison A 8 d.	25/03/1917	26/03/1917
War Diary	Sheet 36 NW 1:20,000	26/03/1917	26/03/1917
War Diary	Blanche Maison A 8 d.	27/03/1917	28/03/1917
War Diary	Maison Blanche		
War Diary	Houplines 36 NW 1:10.000 Le Bizet C 13d	05/04/1917	19/04/1917
War Diary	France Sheet 36 1:40.000 Blanche Maison A 2 d	20/04/1917	28/04/1917
War Diary	Steent-Je S2d	29/04/1917	30/04/1917
War Diary	Sheet 36a Strazeele E 12 C	01/05/1917	03/05/1917
War Diary	Strazeele	04/05/1917	04/05/1917
War Diary	(Map.Hazebrouck 5A) Wallon Cappel	05/05/1917	05/05/1917
War Diary	Quelmes	06/05/1917	06/05/1917
War Diary	Cormette	07/05/1917	09/05/1917
War Diary	Ref. Map Hazebrouck 5A Cormette	10/05/1917	17/05/1917
War Diary	Ebblinghem	18/05/1917	18/05/1917
War Diary	Strazeele	19/05/1917	19/05/1917
War Diary	Ref, Map Sheet 28.S.W.	20/05/1917	24/05/1917
War Diary	T.20.C.3.0	25/05/1917	29/05/1917
War Diary	Sheet 28 S.W. Camp at T 20 C 5.3 Wulverghem	29/05/1917	02/06/1917
War Diary	Wulverghem Sector	03/06/1917	21/06/1917
War Diary	Belgium & France Sheet 28 S 17 C	22/06/1917	22/06/1917
War Diary	Belg & France Sheet 28 S 17 C. Ravelsberg	23/06/1917	23/06/1917
War Diary	Sheet Hazebrouck Ed. 2 1:10.000		
War Diary	Vieux Berquin	24/06/1917	24/06/1917
War Diary	Havers-Kerque	25/06/1917	25/06/1917
War Diary	Rely	26/06/1917	26/06/1917
War Diary	Delette	27/06/1917	27/06/1917
War Diary	Hazebrouck 5a Ed. 2.1:100.000 Delette	28/06/1917	28/06/1917
War Diary	Sheet 1:40.000 Therouanne R.1 Central Delette	29/06/1917	29/06/1917
War Diary	Delette	30/06/1917	01/07/1917
War Diary	Delette Sheet Therouanne 1:40.000 R.1. Central	02/07/1917	05/07/1917
War Diary	Delette	06/07/1917	06/07/1917
War Diary	Sheet Hazebrouck 5a.1:100.000 Tannay	07/07/1917	07/07/1917
War Diary	Halifax Camp Belgium & France Sheet 28 1:40.000 H.18.d.9.1	08/07/1917	08/07/1917
War Diary	Belgium And France Sheet 28 1:40.000		
War Diary	Halifax Camp H.18.d.9.1	09/07/1917	09/07/1917
War Diary	Ypres I 8 C. 25.10	10/07/1917	10/07/1917
War Diary	Ypres Belg & France Sheet 28 1:40.000 I 8 C 2.5 10	10/07/1917	12/07/1917
War Diary	Ypres Belgium And France Sheet 28 1:40.000	13/07/1917	23/07/1917

Type	Description	Date From	Date To
War Diary	Halifax Camp France Sheet 28 1:40.000 H.18.d.9.1	24/07/1917	24/07/1917
War Diary	Reninghelst G.22.C.8.7	25/07/1917	25/07/1917
War Diary	Reninghelst	26/07/1917	28/11/1917
Miscellaneous	Relief Orders. (No. 1)	20/10/1917	20/10/1917
Operation(al) Order(s)	Releif Order No. 2 Appendix 1	31/10/1917	31/10/1917
Operation(al) Order(s)	Relief Order No. 3 Appendix I		
Miscellaneous	Appendix No. 4		
Miscellaneous	Relief Orders Appendix 3		
Operation(al) Order(s)	Relief Order No. 5 Appendix 5	26/11/1917	26/11/1917
War Diary		29/11/1917	28/12/1917
Operation(al) Order(s)	Relief Order No. 6 Appendix 1	08/12/1917	08/12/1917
Miscellaneous	Relief Order No. 7 by Capt J. Best, Commdg 7th Machine Gun Company. Appendix 2	20/12/1917	20/12/1917
Miscellaneous	7th Machine Gun Company Appendix 3		
Miscellaneous	Operation Order No. 9 Appendix 4	26/12/1917	26/12/1917
War Diary		29/12/1917	28/01/1918
War Diary	7th Machine Gun Company Appendix No. 1	31/12/1917	31/12/1917
Miscellaneous	Relief Order No. 10 Appendix No. 2		
Operation(al) Order(s)	Relief Order No. 77 Appendix No. 3	17/01/1918	17/01/1918
Miscellaneous	Relief Orders. Appendix No. 4		
War Diary		29/01/1918	28/02/1918
War Diary	Relief Order No. 12 Appendix No. 1		

No0512244/6

25TH DIVISION
7TH INFY. BDE

7TH MACHINE GUN COY.
JAN 1916-FEB 1918

7th Inf. Bde.

25th Division

7th Bde. MACHINE GUN COY.,

JANUARY, 1916.

7th Rose Machine Gun Co.

Jan
Vol I

WAR DIARY
INTELLIGENCE SUMMARY.

(Erase heading not required.)

Army Form C. 2118.

Instructions regarding War Diaries and Intelligence Summaries are contained in F.S. Regs., Part II. and the Staff Manual respectively. Title pages will be prepared in manuscript.

Place	Date	Hour	Summary of Events and Information	Remarks and references to Appendices
ROESBRUGGE	12/1/16		7th Inf. Bde M.G. Coy officially formed, has 3 in action relieved by 132 in trenches 121 to 127. Coy complete as regards section & transport but short of 4 officers & 12 men. Headqrs in field at PONT D'ACHELLES	Q
"	13/1/16		One horse cast. Mainly sent to hospital. Muddy day	Q
"	14/1/16		Lt Ramsey reported for duty. Wet day very dull	Q
"	15/1/16		Trouble from 2 two gun firing nights of 14-15th on TROIS TILLEULS & Au CHASSEUR CABARET	Q
"	16/1/16		Fine clear day. One gun firing intermittently on LA POTTERIE Remainder on LA HUTTE.	Q
"	17/1/16		Clear day. Front quiet	Q
"	18/1/16		Los 192 3 in relieved by 3 x 4 in in the trenches.	Q
"	19/1/16		4 guns in action on open land behind LAWRENCE Fm. Fire opened at 4.30 P.M. on roads & CTs round PONT ROUGE to assist further attacking LE TOUQUET SALIENT & prevent German supports coming up. Fire ceased at 5.15 P.M. Rounds fired. 3000 Retaliatory shelling along held on wipes line but no damage.	Q

WAR DIARY or INTELLIGENCE SUMMARY

Army Form C. 2118.

Place	Date	Hour	Summary of Events and Information	Remarks and references to Appendices
PLOEGSTEERT	20/1/16		Clear day. Everything quiet.	
	21/1/16		Clear day. Officers of 27th Bde M.G. Coy interviewed the kitchen.	
	22/1/16		Showery day. Has 30 s/m. Handgun & transport moved by road to temporary billets at A.4.d.1.2. Sheet 36.	
LA BECQUE	23/1/16		S/m. & returned in billets by section of 27/6 Bde M.G. Coy, in relief by 27/6 Bde M.G. Coy.	
"			Relief my est. S/m moved to billets at 4 P.M.	
"	24/1/16		Very fine day. Cleaning guns, cleaning spare parts.	
"	25/1/16		" " Examining & filling belts.	
Mt à VAPEUR	26/1/16		Coy moved to Rest billets at X.24.c.1. Sheet 27. Relief taken over from 26th Bde M.G. Coy.	
Sheet 27 X.24.c.1	27/1/16		Clear day. Transport teams in hand. General cleaning up.	
"	28/1/16		" . Started training when fine day.	
"	29/1/16		Windy day. Training. Walk from .	
"	30/1/16		Very windy. Church parade at 9 A.M.	

7th Inf. Bde.

25th Division.

7th Bde. MACHINE GUN COY.,

FEBRUARY, 1916.

Army Form C. 2118.

WAR DIARY
or
INTELLIGENCE SUMMARY.
(Erase heading not required.)

Instructions regarding War Diaries and Intelligence Summaries are contained in F. S. Regs., Part II. and the Staff Manual respectively. Title pages will be prepared in manuscript.

Place	Date	Hour	Summary of Events and Information	Remarks and references to Appendices
BAILLEUL	31/1/16		Route march without transport 8 miles	
"	1/2/16		Training to programme	
"	2/2/16		" Firing on range	
"	3/2/16		Route march, 12 miles without packs	
"	4/2/16		Training to programme. Range firing	
"	5/2/16		"	
"	6/2/16		Church parade in morning. Walk old breastworks bullets & clearing up	
"	7/2/16		Bde route march. 8 mile.	
"	8/2/16		All trains returned from overhaul. Training to programme	
"	9/2/16		Training to programme. Range firing.	
"	10/2/16		"	
"	11/2/16		Route march with guns	
"	12/2/16		Training to programme	
"	13/2/16		Church parade	
"	14/2/16		Training to programme Bde under 4 hours notice to move	
"	15/2/16		" hours to move withdrawn	

T134. W1. W708—776. 500000. 4/15. Sir J. C. & S.

WAR DIARY or INTELLIGENCE SUMMARY.

Army Form C. 2118.

Instructions regarding War Diaries and Intelligence Summaries are contained in F. S. Regs., Part II. and the Staff Manual respectively. Title pages will be prepared in manuscript.

(Erase heading not required.)

Place	Date	Hour	Summary of Events and Information	Remarks and references to Appendices
BAILLEUL	16/1/16		Received notice at 6am that Bttn was ordered to move from OUDERSTEENE at 11 am to support of 9th Divn at RAMARIN. Bttn rode-ment in gale with snow storms. Snow busting low. LLD	
"	17/1/16		Training to programme	
"	18/1/16		" " rang firing	
"	19/1/16		" "	
"	20/1/16		Church parade. Aeroplane came over BAILLEUL. Training to programme.	
"	21/1/16		" "	
"	22/1/16		Brigade attack scheme. Attack developed in snowstorm which completely cut off view.	
"	23/1/16		Found snow covered hard frost. Training indoors.	
"	24/1/16		Training under cover.	
"	25/1/16		Training to programme. Divl attack scheme dismissed on gound of ground beginning to clear. Bns - Bgs in 4 hours notice to proceed by rail.	
"	27/1/16		Church parade. Visited by BOE trenches in front of ARMENTIÈRES.	

Army Form C. 2118.

WAR DIARY
or
INTELLIGENCE SUMMARY.
(Erase heading not required.)

Instructions regarding War Diaries and Intelligence Summaries are contained in F. S. Regs., Part II. and the Staff Manual respectively. Title pages will be prepared in manuscript.

Place	Date	Hour	Summary of Events and Information	Remarks and references to Appendices
Bailleul	28/7/16		All gone on weekend preparatory to move	

7th Inf. Bde.

25th Division

7th Bde. MACHINE GUN COY.,

MARCH, 1916.

7th INFANTRY BDE
25th DIVISION.

10th BATTN CHESHIRE REGIMENT

6th OCTOBER 1916

XV. 3

7 Bde M.G. Coy.

Vol III

Army Form C. 2118.

WAR DIARY
or
INTELLIGENCE SUMMARY.
(Erase heading not required.)

Instructions regarding War Diaries and Intelligence Summaries are contained in F. S. Regs., Part II. and the Staff Manual respectively. Title pages will be prepared in manuscript.

Place	Date	Hour	Summary of Events and Information	Remarks and references to Appendices
BAILLEUL	29/9/16			
	1/9/16		Route march in morning – 10 miles. 8PM received orders to turn out at once. Our starting point at 9.10. Reached pt. congln. him out at 9.15 P.M.; marched thro METEREN & back to billets.	
	2/9/16		Going weather – raining hard; cleaning up in billets	
	3/9/16		Raining hard. Entire in billets. Pte PEARCE No. 18066 went to F.A. accidentally wounded by rifle shot.	
	4/9/16		Fine day. Training to programme	
	5/9/16		Snowing hard	
	6/9/16		Turned out 8.30 for Bde Route march, turned back owing to condition of frozen roads	
	7/9/16		Ditto	
	8/9/16		Marched off at 8 a.m. for Bde route march. Route STRAZEELE – BORRE – FLÊTRE – METEREN back to billets.	
	9/9/16		Cleaning up preparatory to move.	
	10/9/16		Left billets at 8.15 a.m. & marched via NEUF BERQUIN – MERVILLE –

Army Form C. 2118.

WAR DIARY
or
~~INTELLIGENCE SUMMARY.~~
(Erase heading not required.)

VII

Instructions regarding War Diaries and Intelligence Summaries are contained in F. S. Regs., Part II. and the Staff Manual respectively. Title pages will be prepared in manuscript.

Place	Date	Hour	Summary of Events and Information	Remarks and references to Appendices
ROBECQ	10/3/16		ROBECQ to billets at HOLLANDERIE, one mile NW of ROBECQ	
	11/3/16		Left billets at 7.45 a.m. & marched via BUSNES – LILLERS – PERNIN – VALHUON to billets at BRIAS arriving at 2 p.m.	
BRIAS	12/3/16		Fine weather – cleaning up billets.	
"	13/3/16		" – firing on range	
"	14/3/16		" "	
"	15/3/16		Cleaning up preparatory to move	
"	16/3/16		Left billets at 6.45 a.m. marched via OSTERVILLE – MARQUAY – LIGNY – AVERDOINGT to PENIN where billeted in old French billets.	
PENIN	17/3/16		Cleaning up billets.	
"	18/3/16		Ditto.	
"	19/3/16		Church parade with 3RD WORCESTERSHIRE REGT	
"	20/3/16		Firing on range	
"	21/3/16		" "	
"	22/3/16		" "	
"	23/3/16		Weather very dull. Cleaning up billets. Two Officers and 8 Company commanders visited front of MT ST ELOY.	

WAR DIARY
or
INTELLIGENCE SUMMARY

Army Form C. 2118.

Place	Date	Hour	Summary of Events and Information	Remarks and references to Appendices
PERNE	24/3/16		Snowing heavily. Two Officers reached Corps line in front of M= St. Eloi.	
"	25/3/16		Sunny day. Route march 10 miles @	
"	26/3/16		Heavy wind storm @	
"	27/3/16		O.C. left on leave. 2 i/c Roper in charge. Firing on range. G.O.C. Division inspected section firing, and required transport drivers to be trained in M.G. Staff S. 2 arrived MR	
"	28/3/16		Transport drivers firing on range. Gun drill & fire control practised, whole company in line, in anticipation of inspection by C. in C. MR	
"	29/3/16		General clean up for inspection. Instructional parade for drivers + batmen MR	
"	30/3/16		Company parade on range. Firing with all guns in line. Instruction of batmen as before MR	
"	31/3/16		Company paraded on range at 11 am for C. in C's inspection, but returned to billets at 2 pm. the C. in C. being unable to inspect from lack of time. Notes fine. MR	

7th Infantry Bde
25th DIVISION

7th Bde. MACHINE GUN COY.,

1?   APRIL, 1916.

Army Form C. 2118.

WAR DIARY
or
INTELLIGENCE SUMMARY.
(Erase heading not required.)

Instructions regarding War Diaries and Intelligence Summaries are contained in F. S. Regs., Part II. and the Staff Manual respectively. Title pages will be prepared in manuscript.

Place	Date	Hour	Summary of Events and Information	Remarks and references to Appendices
Field	1.4.16		On rest billets at PENIN. Training to programme.	
	5.4.16		Brigade sports branch round brigade area, for inspection by G.O.C. Corps.	
	6.4.16		O.C. returned from leave.	
	11.4.16		Brigade HQrs: HQ moved to AUBIGNY. O.C. Coy moved to billets in BETHENCOURT near TINCQUES.	
	11-20.4.16		Training to programme. Weather stormy. Officers reconnoitred trenches + positions held by 139th M.G. Coy. north of NEUVILLE St VAAST.	
	20.4.16		Coy moved into trenches to relieve 139th Coy. 3 sections moved into line, 1 section and Head quarters remained in billets at MONT ST ELOY. Considerable mining + bombing activity. Disposition of guns: 5 in avalanche line (P. 73, 75, 77, 78 + 79) 6 in support.	
	24 + 4.16		No. 2 section relieved No. 3 in line — supplying indirect fire.	
	25.4.16		1 casualty from piece of shrapnel. No. 3 returned to billets at Mt St ELOY.	
	26.4.16		Accident with trench mortar.	
	28.4.16		No. 3 section relieved No. 4 section in line. No. 4 section returned to billets. Work on trench, cleaning, draining + deepening trenches. Work on emplacements. Construction of a splinter proof shelter + indirect fire position.	

D.A.G
3rd Echelon
BEF

73.

SECRET

Herewith is sent original war diary for April 1916 of the 7th Machine Gun Company

M R M°C Lieut
for O.C. 7th M.G. Coy

30-4-16

7th Inf. Bde.

25th Division

7th Bde. MACHINE GUN COY.,

M A Y, 1 9 1 6.

WAR DIARY
or
INTELLIGENCE SUMMARY.
(Erase heading not required.)

Army Form C. 2118.

Place	Date	Hour	Summary of Events and Information	Remarks and references to Appendices
Mt St Eloy	1/5/16		Line quiet except the exception of bombing. The emplacements under construction.	Ⓐ
"	2/5/16		" " Indirect fire on LA FOLIE slopes	Ⓐ
"	3/5/16		" " PETIT VIMY slow retaliation by 3" H.E.	Ⓐ
"	4/5/16		Very quiet, a little shelling with shrapnel no damage done	Ⓐ
"	5/5/16		Indirect fire on tracks leading away from LA FOLIE WOOD	Ⓐ
"	6/5/16		Occasional shelling of CENTRAL & LOOP DUMP	Ⓐ
"	7/5/16		Day quiet. Enfilement on P78.S2 finished & occupied.	Ⓐ
"	8/5/16		Day quiet, some bombing after dark. Indirect fire on LA FOLIE slopes	Ⓐ
"	9/5/16		Day quiet, some bombing at night.	Ⓐ
"	10/5/16		Occasional shelling of CENTRAL; some tracks behind LA FOLIE WOOD provided retaliation.	Ⓐ
"	11/5/16		Day quiet. Indirect fire on GIVENCHY.	Ⓐ
"	12/5/16		" " Indirect fire on GIVENCHY.	Ⓐ
"	13/5/16		Heavy shelling of P76.S2, dugout damaged a man shaken but no serious wounds	Ⓐ
"	14/5/16		Heavy shelling of our support line but no damage done.	Ⓐ
"			After a heavy shelling Germans made a bombing attack & captured BROADMARSH CRATER in spite of counter attacks by 10TH CHESHIRES.	Ⓐ
"	15/5/16		A party of 8TH L.N.L occupied BROADMARSH CRATER at 9.15 am	Ⓐ

WAR DIARY or INTELLIGENCE SUMMARY

Army Form C. 2118.

Place	Date	Hour	Summary of Events and Information	Remarks and references to Appendices
Mt St ELOY.	15/5/16		cont. During attack our guns were firing to rt. & lt. flank & using O.T.M to keep down enemy fire as much as possible.	
"	16/5/16		Enemy started to drop very much more bombs on P.79.	@
"	17/5/16		No. 10336 Pte EDWARDS hit by shrapnel and two bombs hit. Dug-out @ ammunition bombs on P.79. P.78 enemy's trench in flames.	@
"	18/5/16		Shelling appears to be registration purposes OH firs on PETIT VIMY. @ fire guns & ours in P.78 harried by fire of 6" HE shells.	@
"	19/5/16		No.18017 Pte GREGORY killed. No.18059 Corpl LIGHT - No.18077 Pte DENTON No.7516 Pte HAGGAR, No.10999. Pte SAUNDERSON wounded.	@
"	20/5/16		Guns dug out at night - from strong box uncovered. Intense enemy bombardment started at 3.30 p.m. at 8.0 p.m. enemy came over on P.79 & the next Brigade front on left. guns in P.79 fell back into P.79.S. & with gun strong-team held up attack until L.C.R. guns were put out of action by shrapnel. L.Cpl BROPHY, Lanborough our left guns - two wounded men across the open under very heavy fire. Gun in P.78 opened fire on attack & caused heavy casualties.	@

WAR DIARY
or
INTELLIGENCE SUMMARY.
(Erase heading not required.)

Army Form C. 2118.

Place	Date	Hour	Summary of Events and Information	Remarks and references to Appendices
Mt ST ELOY	21/5/16		contd) in the flank of the attack which in consequence did not reach P78. Two rear guns were placed in OLD QUARRIES but were not req'd.	Lewenthi Appendix I
"	22/5/16		Germans held apart of P79 & CENTRAL as far as the junction of P79. Situation on left brigade front uncertain. Two guns placed in TERRIER to watch flank.	
"	23/5/16		Quiet day - occasional shelling by our own guns. At 8.25 p.m. 3RD WORCESTER REGT counter-attacked on left in conjunction with attack by left Brigade (which did not take place) all P79 was reoccupied but in consequence of enfilade left flank had to be swung back. The attack was supported by No.5 gun firing across the front from in P78 B.2. rammer & shoot hit from a 6" H.E. gun smashed up 9 team knocked out - Killed - No 18094 Pte RUDGE, No 18095 Pte POOLE. No 10339 Pte GRIFFITHS. 1 - wounded No 10059 Pte JOHNSTONE	
"	24/5/16		Occasional heavy shelling otherwise situation very quiet. Two guns brought up & placed in PYLONES at junction with CENTRAL.	

Army Form C. 2118.

WAR DIARY
or
INTELLIGENCE SUMMARY.
(Erase heading not required.)

Instructions regarding War Diaries and Intelligence Summaries are contained in F. S. Regs., Part II. and the Staff Manual respectively. Title pages will be prepared in manuscript.

Place	Date	Hour	Summary of Events and Information	Remarks and references to Appendices
Mt St Eloi	25/5/16		Situation quiet. R.E. shot work on two new emplacements.	Q
"	26/5/16		very quiet. Broken gun replaced from reserve.	Q
"	27/5/16		A camouflet was blown up by enemy without result.	Q
"	28/5/16		Situation very quiet. Two enemy planes driven off by M.G.	Q
"	29/4/16		mounted in Quarries. Occasional shelling of enemy situation seen.	Q
"	30/5/16		One gun of relieving Co. 152nd M.G.C. sent in.	Q
"	31/5/16		Remaining guns of relieving Co. sent in to take over.	Q

7th Bde M.G. Coy.

Casualties in Action

6250	Pte Smith	Wounded	26.4.16
15195	" Collier	"	26.4.16
10336	" Edwards	Died from Wounds	17.5.16
18119	L/Cpl Abraham	Killed in action	21.5.16
18057	Sgt Rochester J.H.	Wounded	21.5.16
18063	Pte Burton G.H.	"	21.5.16
18120	" O'Hare J	"	21.5.16
18118	" Harte S.	"	21.5.16
18123	" Cunningham J.	"	21.5.16
18137	" Gibson W.G.	"	21.5.16
12116	" Mitchell A	"	21.5.16
18114	" Stevenson J	"	21.5.16
12436	" Hudson W	"	22.5.16
11279	Cpl Goodacre C.C.	slightly wounded	24.5.16
18061	L/C Tucker D.	"	24.5.16

Index 4/0 1.

7th Inf. Bde.

25th Division

7th Bde. MACHINE GUN COY.,

JUNE, 1916.

WAR DIARY
or
INTELLIGENCE SUMMARY.
(Erase heading not required.)

Army Form C. 2118.

7 Bde M.G. Coy   Vol 6

Place	Date	Hour	Summary of Events and Information	Remarks and references to Appendices
Mt St ELOI.	1/6/16		All guns brought out in the evening last evening to heavy shell barrage on the BETHUNE RD. relief was delayed by 3 hours	
	2/6/16		Left Mt St ELOI at 8 p.m. & marched via VILLERS BRULIN & FREVILLIERS to HERLIN LE VERT, arriving at 2.30 a.m. 3/6/16.	
HERLIN LE VERT	3/6/16		Installed in billets at HERLIN LE VERT	
	4/6/16		General overhaul of equipment & kit.	
G 2, I 7 Rd LENS Sheet No 11	5/6/16 6/6/16 7/6/16 8/6/16		General training – weather cold & wet.	
	9/6/16		Inspection of Bde. by B.D.C.	
	10/6/16		Brigade Field Day, attack on 3rd line of positions.	
	11/6/16		General training – weather very wet.	
	12/6/16		Quiet Field Day	
AVEROINGT	13/6/16		Left HERLIN LE VERT at 8 a.m. & marched via CHELERS & TINQUES to AVEROINGT, arriving at 12.30 p.m. & billeting	
F 2, 1, 51.				

Army Form C. 2118.

WAR DIARY
or
INTELLIGENCE SUMMARY.
(Erase heading not required.)

Instructions regarding War Diaries and Intelligence Summaries are contained in F. S. Regs., Part II. and the Staff Manual respectively. Title pages will be prepared in manuscript.

XVI

Place	Date	Hour	Summary of Events and Information	Remarks and references to Appendices
BEAUVOIS 1EME SHEET 1/10,000 D4,4,8	14/6/16		Left AVEROINGT at 8AM & moved via MAIZIERES to BEAUVOIR & billets arriving at 1.30 pm	
"	15/6/16		Training in billets 2/Lt BOWSTER reported	
"	16/6/16		Left BEAUVOIR at 10.30 pm & moved via TOARLY & DECOCHES to LONGUEVILLETTE arriving in billets at 2 am Re 17/6	
LONGUEVILLETTE (D5, 36)	17/6/16		Left LONGUEVILLETTE at 11.15 pm & moved via FIENVILLERS & CANAPLES to billets in HALLOY-LES-PERNOIS arriving at 3.15am on Re 18/6/16	
HALLOY LES PERNOIS (C6, 46)	18/6/16		Training in billets	
"	19/6/16		"	
"	20/6/16		Training in billets	
"	21/6/16		" Lt RAMSAY left for transport course at HAVRE	
"	22/6/16		"	
"	23/6/16		"	
"	24/6/16		All guns fired & sights tested	
"	25/6/16		Sunday Church Parade 11 am	

WAR DIARY
~~INTELLIGENCE SUMMARY~~

Army Form C. 2118.

Place	Date	Hour	Summary of Events and Information	Remarks and references to Appendices
HALLOY-LES-PERNOIS	25/4/16		Training	
	27/6/16		Attack scheme before G.S.O.I. 25th Div. Q. Regt at 11 PM & marched via TALMAS & HAVRS to PUCHEVILLERS where billeted at 4 a.m.	
PUCHEVILLERS	28/6/16		Training	
"	29/6/16		Training	
"	30/6/16			

7th Bde.
25th Div.

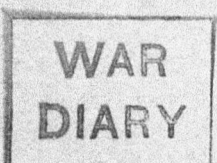

7th MACHINE GUN COMPANY.

JULY 1916

List of casualties attached.

WAR DIARY
or
INTELLIGENCE SUMMARY.

Army Form C. 2118.

7th M.G. Coy.
M G Coy
Vol 1

(Erase heading not required.)

Place	Date	Hour	Summary of Events and Information	Remarks and references to Appendices
SOMME	night 30June 1July		moved to Lealvillers into Billets. MR	
	1 July	8 pm	moved to Huts in VARENNES MR	
	2 "	1.30 pm	moved to Huts in HEDAUVILLE MR	
	"	10.30 pm	" assembly trenches in AVELUY WOOD MR	
	3 "		In AVELUY WOOD. 8 p.m. Nos. 1 + 4 sections went into line opposite AUTHUILLE in relief of sections of 14th Company. MR	
	4 "		No. 2 section into line. H.Q. + No. 3 section into reserve dugouts in AUTHUILLE MR	
	5 "	8 pm	1st WILT Regt supported by Company guns attacked gaining further ground in the LEIPSIC REDOUBT MR	
	6 "	1.30am	Further progress in LEIPSIC REDOUBT MR	
	MIDNIGHT 7th/8th		Company relieved by 146th Company. Returned to assembly trenches in AVELUY WOOD MR	
	8 "	9 a	moved to BIVOUAC on TARA HILL on ALBERT-LABOISSELLE road MR	
	9 "		Officers reconnoitred positions at LABOISSELLE MR	
	10 "	2.30 pm	3 sections into line to relieve 74th Company. L.D. LAINES up, not strong enemy counter attack in C.T. from BOISSELLE toward POZIÈRES. No. 2 section fired into attack at 800 range. MR	

Army Form C. 2118.

WAR DIARY
or
INTELLIGENCE SUMMARY.
(Erase heading not required.)

Instructions regarding War Diaries and Intelligence Summaries are contained in F. S. Regs., Part II. and the Staff Manual respectively. Title pages will be prepared in manuscript.

Place	Date	Hour	Summary of Events and Information	Remarks and references to Appendices
SOMME	11th		Guns firing into OVILLERS - LA BOISSELLE in support of bombing attacks. mm	
	12th-13th	Midnight	10th CHESHIRE Regt. occupied enemy trenches on BAPAUME Road at point 66, 1000 yards S.W. of POZIERES. 2 Coys of No 2 section moved up to this point across country. mm	
	13th-14th		These guns relieved by No 3 section. Further attack on OVILLERS by 7th & 75th Bdes. mm	
	14th-15th		were beating progress by 7th & 75th Bdes in OVILLERS, supported by fire of Coy. mm	
	15th	6 pm	Company relieved by 7th Coy. M.G. moved to Bivouac by ruin ANCRE outside ALBERT. mm	
	16th	9.30 pm	moved to rest billets in FORCEVILLE mm	
	17th		In billets. Guns & equipment reorganized mm	
	18th	8 am	marched through BEAUQUESNE to billets in BEAUVAL mm	
	19th		In billets mm	
	20th	noon	marched to huts in Bois de WARNIMONT near AUTHIE mm	
	21st & 22nd		In huts. Range practice & parades. mm	
	23rd	10.15 am	moved to MAILLY-MAILLET into huts. Officers & NCOs reconnoitred line mm	
	24th	2 pm	3 sections into line at HAMEL in relief of 86th Coy. mm	

Army Form C. 2118.

WAR DIARY
or
INTELLIGENCE SUMMARY.
(Erase heading not required.)

Instructions regarding War Diaries and Intelligence Summaries are contained in F.S. Regs., Part II. and the Staff Manual respectively. Title pages will be prepared in manuscript.

Place	Date	Hour	Summary of Events and Information	Remarks and references to Appendices
Somme	25th 26th 27th 28th 29th		In line at HAMEL. Situation quiet.	

7th — M. G. Coy
Casualties

18169	Pte Harrison H	4·7·16	Wounded
2nd Lt	C. D. Oakes	5·7·16	"
	C R Leary	5·7·16	"
18156	Sgt Roden C	5·7·16	"
18085	" Walton G	5·7·16	"
18131	Pte Quinn J	5·7·16	"
18130	" Lennox J	5·7·16	"
12521	" Loake F	5·7·16	"
18134	" Jamieson P	5·7·16	"
8985	" Ashbourne W	5·7·16	"
14975	" Watts F	5·7·16	Killed
26427	" Young G	5·7·16	Wounded At Duty
18109	Sgt O'Rourke J	8·7·16	Killed
1330	Pte Wright G	8·7·16	Wounded
4325	" Cox A	8·7·16	"
18056	Sgt Petty C	10·7·16	"
12212	Pte Westbrooke G	10·7·16	"
18078	" Perritt F	10·7·16	"
18079	" Denton H	10·7·16	"
18065	" Scott F	10·7·16	At Duty
18164	" Shelly J	12·7·16	Wounded
21161	" Fitzsimmons W	12·7·16	"
18159	" Hewitt F	13·7·16	Killed
8170	" Hull A	13·7·16	Wounded
18076	" Stone C	13·7·16	"
18077	" Payne C G	13·7·16	"
2nd Lt	Sheatfield	11·7·16	"

7th Brigade.
25th Division.

7th BRIGADE.

MACHINE GUN COMPANY

AUGUST 1 9 1 6

Original
Army Form C. 2118.
Vol 8

1/1st M.G. Coy.

WAR DIARY
or
INTELLIGENCE SUMMARY.
(Erase heading not required.)

Instructions regarding War Diaries and Intelligence Summaries are contained in F. S. Regs., Part II. and the Staff Manual respectively. Title pages will be prepared in manuscript.

Place	Date	Hour	Summary of Events and Information	Remarks and references to Appendices
Somme	1-8-16			
	2 -			
	3 -		In trenches north of R. ANCRE at HAMEL. Weather fine, situation quiet. MR.	
	4 -			
	5 -			
	6 -			
	7 -			
	7.8.16		Relieved by 18th M.G. Coy. To billets in BERTRANCOURT, entraining. MR	
	8 -		In billets. Training. MR	
	9 -			
	10.8.16		Moved to billets in VAUCHELLES-LÈS-AUTHIE, in place of 1st Guards M.G. Coy. MR	
	11		In billets. Training. MR	
	12			
	13.8.16		1 section attached for anti-aircraft duties at PUCHEVILLERS and HETTING AUTHEUX. MR	

WAR DIARY
or
INTELLIGENCE SUMMARY.
(Erase heading not required.)

Army Form C. 2118.

Instructions regarding War Diaries and Intelligence Summaries are contained in F. S. Regs., Part II. and the Staff Manual respectively. Title pages will be prepared in manuscript.

Place	Date	Hour	Summary of Events and Information	Remarks and references to Appendices
SOMME	15.8.16		Coy less two sections moved to PUCHEVILLERS T. WALG mr	
	16 -		In billets. mr	
	17 -			
	18.8.16		Coy less one two sections moved to HEDAUVILLE.	
	19.8.16		Coy moved into trenches at LEIPSIC SALIENT in relief of 1/4th by Headquarters in AUTHUILLE. mr.	
	20 -		In trenches. Artillery activity. mr.	
	21 -			
	22			
	23	noon	attack on trg 48. Bdes on right mr	
		6pm	further attack by same in conjunction with WARTS mr	
	24	4.10 pm	attack by WILTS & WORCESTERS on HINDENBURG TRENCH. 4 guns placed in captured trench & consolidate. Capt. J.A RUTHERFORD (commanding) & 2/LT R.W. BIRD killed. Capt Rutherford was killed by a stray bullet when junction had started, while reconnoitring in the LEIPSIC SALIENT. 2 Lieut BIRD was	

WAR DIARY or INTELLIGENCE SUMMARY

Army Form C. 2118.

Place	Date	Hour	Summary of Events and Information	Remarks and references to Appendices
	24.8.16 (contd)		killed by shrapnel s/L. organising the defence of the captured trenches with the greatest skill & bravery. After reconnoitring the position he found the two guns details had been put out of action by shell fire. He brought up another Lewis gun, & found a Gun & Team & German ammunition & one of the guns had just put out of action. He made several journeys to the captured position under heavy barrages & himself carried up a gun & ammunition. He was assisted by Sergt TAYLOR, who returned from the 2 teams put out of action. The remaining two teams held off to consolidate men taken into position successfully & enabled TPR command & HINDENBURG trench stopped by barrage.	Lieut W. ROSCOE 7th R. N. R. Sergeant TAYLOR 2nd R.
	25.8.16	7.30 p.m.	German counter-attack on HINDENBURG trench stopped by barrage.	25th Coy. M.R.
	26.8.16	8.30 p.m.	to guns in HINDENBURG trench relieved by guns of 75th Coy. M.R.	
	27.8.16	9 a.m.	remainder of guns & headquarters relieved by 75th Coy. to billets in HEDAUVILLE 75th R.	
	28.8.16		To billets in BOUZINCOURT 75th R.	

Army Form C. 2118.

WAR DIARY
or
INTELLIGENCE SUMMARY.
(Erase heading not required.)

Instructions regarding War Diaries and Intelligence Summaries are contained in F. S. Regs., Part II. and the Staff Manual respectively. Title pages will be prepared in manuscript.

Place	Date	Hour	Summary of Events and Information	Remarks and references to Appendices
SOMME	29.8.16		Capt. H.D. SPARK, 153rd Coy. TMB on command from Lieut ROSCOE	

7th. INFANTRY BDE.

25th. DIVISION

7th. MACHINE GUN COMPANY

SEPTEMBER 1916.

WAR DIARY
or
INTELLIGENCE SUMMARY
(Erase heading not required.)

Army Form C. 2118.

28 vol 9
2/7 MG Coy

Place	Date	Hour	Summary of Events and Information	Remarks and references to Appendices
In the Field	1916 30th		On the 28th our guns under Lieut Ramsay went up & reported to 7th MG Coy to be under their command and are still there. Rearranging limbers gunteams &c. The remainder of the Company are in billets at BOUZINCOURT.	
	31st		Six guns still in the line. Continued work on hilts &c with men out.	
Sept A.A.C.	1st		In afternoon six gun teams under 2nd Lieut Lovel went up to relieve our teams in the line.	
	2nd		Ceremonial drill with men out of trenches. 6 guns still in	
	3rd		Church parade at BOUSINCOURT	
	4th		Making out lots of deficiencies still at BOUSINCOURT	
	5th		Moved via HEDAUVILLE, VARENNES, to LEAVILLERS	
	6th		Six guns left in trenches under 96th Brigade rejoined us at LEAVILLERS at 6pm today	
	7th		Moved to ARCQUEVES where we stayed in tents till the 10th. During this time did some M.G. firing and revolver practice.	
	10th		Marched via RAINCHEVAL TERRAMESNEL to GEZAINCOURT where we are billeted	
	11th		Marched via HEM LE MEILLARD to RIBEAUCOURT where we are billeted	
	12th		Marched via BEAUMETZ & LONGVILLERS to COULINVILLERS	
	13th to 15		General training in M.G. work including concealment of guns, flattering	

Army Form C. 2118.

WAR DIARY
or
INTELLIGENCE SUMMARY.
(Erase heading not required.)

Instructions regarding War Diaries and Intelligence Summaries are contained in F.S. Regs., Part II. and the Staff Manual respectively. Title pages will be prepared in manuscript.

Place	Date	Hour	Summary of Events and Information	Remarks and references to Appendices
RIBEAUCOURT	16th		Moved back to RIBEAUCOURT along with T.M. battery and took over original billets.	
	17 to 23rd		Training in M.G. work and army quite a lot of firing had all No's 1, 2's out for revolver practice. Did advancing motor and moving into action with all 16 guns in line on 22nd. Company was inspected by Brigadier.	
"	24th		Two guns proceeded under Lt Laing to COULONVILLERS to test emplacements made by R.E.s. Church service held in hut, chevarone Lane Canteen, at 4 p.m.	
GEZAINCOURT	25th		Moved to GEZAINCOURT and stayed night in former billets.	
ARQUEVES	26		Moved to ARQUEVES and on arriving in billets subject on 2 hours notice to move.	
"	27/28th		General cleaning up materials &c	
HEDAUVILLE	29th		Moved up to HEDAUVILLE. C.O. went up to see trenches and make arrangements with 33rd M.G. Coy for relieving them tomorrow.	
	30th		Going up in afternoon to relieve 33rd M.G. Coy.	

Douglas Wyatt
A/Captain O/C
O.C. 1st Machine Gun Coy

Sutterfield

7th Inf. Bde.

25th Division

7th Bde. MACHINE GUN COY.,

OCTOBER, 1916.

Army Form C. 2118.

Vol 10

7th M.G. Coy

WAR DIARY
or
~~INTELLIGENCE SUMMARY.~~

(Erase heading not required.)

Instructions regarding War Diaries and Intelligence Summaries are contained in F. S. Regs., Part II. and the Staff Manual respectively. Title pages will be prepared in manuscript.

Place	Date	Hour	Summary of Events and Information	Remarks and references to Appendices
X 2 a central	30-9-16	8 p.m.	Have taken over from 33rd Machine Gun Coy 11th Division and have 4 guns in HESSIAN TRENCH (front line) under 2nd Lieut Maddison. Two in ZOLLERN & two in SCHWABEN of No 3 Section. Eight in Skyline Trench doing overhead fire on ground sunken road behind STUFF REDOUBT. Fired 5,000 rounds	
do	1-10-16	8 p.m.	Sent four guns of No 2 Section back to transport lines to rest. At 3.15 p.m. carried out OVERHEAD fire on points R20 b 9.4, R21 a 1.2, R21 a 1.2, R21 a 9.5 & R21 a 8.1 & R21 a 6.10 along sunken road, from positions in Skyline Trench to assist Canadian Division on our right, in an attack. One gun out of action as patch on barrel casing has given way. Fired in all 12,000 rounds. During the day kept up fire on ground, behind high ground, towards Grandcourt. Personally reconnoitered all trenches and gun positions and moved two guns from HESSIAN TRENCH into South edge of STUFF REDOUBT as 75th M.G. Coy have withdrawn two they had there. Some heavy shelling during the day.	
do	2-10-16	8 p.m.	Day has been fairly quiet. We were to attack STUFF REDOUBT (north edge) & take points R21 a 80 – 11 -12, R20 b 9.4. at 3.30 p.m. but owing to bad weather which still continues it has been postponed. Went up during forenoon and made	

Army Form C. 2118.

WAR DIARY
or
INTELLIGENCE SUMMARY.
(Erase heading not required.)

Instructions regarding War Diaries and Intelligence Summaries are contained in F. S. Regs., Part II. and the Staff Manual respectively. Title pages will be prepared in manuscript.

Place	Date	Hour	Summary of Events and Information	Remarks and references to Appendices
X 2 a central	2-10-16	8 pm	All arrangements two guns in South of Redoubt were to move up to the North edge of STUFF REDOUBT on its being captured so as to defend the inside flanks of our infantry. Other guns are doing overhead direct fire. Rounds fired during the day sweeping ridge towards Grandcourt 5,000 rounds.	
do	3-10-16	8 pm	Weather was very bad during the forenoon but cleared up in afternoon. Trenches are very dirty. Gunners overhead fire on Unkentood communication trenches at STUFF REDOUBT. Carried out following relief during forenoon. No 1 Section from Skyline trench to Hessian trench. Stuff Redoubt (front line) No 2 Section from transport field to Zollern and Schwaben trench. No 3 Section from Schwaben & Zollern trench to Skyline trench. No 4 Section to transport field. At 4.30 pm our heavy guns bombarded Stuff Redoubt North edge & trenches in vicinity. We did overhead fire from Skyline firing trench and from Schwaben trench on Grandcourt firing during the night continuously.	
do	4-10-16	8 pm	Raining all morning cleared up in the afternoon. No 1 Section's two guns in Stuff Redoubt were continuously shelled during the night, artillery slackened at about 6 am. Communication trench from Zollern trench to Hessian trench was being shelled during the morning until	

WAR DIARY
or
INTELLIGENCE SUMMARY.
(Erase heading not required.)

Army Form C. 2118.

Place	Date	Hour	Summary of Events and Information	Remarks and references to Appendices
X 2.a. central	4/9/16	8 pm	H.E. extensively. Our artillery put a barrage on ground behind STUFF REDOUBT, we co-operated. Firing was carried out by two guns in SCHWABEN TRENCH on GRANDCOURT. Visited all guns during morning, trenches were very wet & muddy. The 4 guns in SKYLINE TRENCH continued overhead fire on Sunken Road and round behind STUFF REDOUBT.	
-Do-	5/9/16	8 pm	The weather has much improved, steady wind blowing from south west. Continued firing on GRANDCOURT & trenches north of STUFF REDOUBT, using 10,000 rounds. Put a barrage from SKYLINE TRENCH on SCHWABEN REDOUBT which we have enfiladed and where enemy were seen, expending to the morning fired 2500 rounds. At 2 p.m. a shell exploded in SCHWABEN TRENCH over gun, wounding 3 men.	
-Do-	6/9/16	8 pm	Continued firing on bombardment & vicinity of STUFF REDOUBT. Weather still fair. Enemy were shelling fairly heavily. K. Rennay was slightly wounded and the G.O. slightly gassed in the afternoon.	
-Do-	7/9/16	8 pm	Went round the line, not much enemy shelling. Weather much better. Received B.O.O. for attack on STUFF REDOUBT by 10th Cheshires, laid & fatal gun in SKYLINE TRENCH.	

Army Form C. 2118.

WAR DIARY
or
INTELLIGENCE SUMMARY.
(Erase heading not required.)

Instructions regarding War Diaries and Intelligence Summaries are contained in F. S. Regs., Part II. and the Staff Manual respectively. Title pages will be prepared in manuscript.

Place	Date	Hour	Summary of Events and Information	Remarks and references to Appendices
X22 central	8/10/16	8 pm	Attack cancelled owing to weather which is very bad. Considerable enemy shell fire in SKYLINE TRENCH	
-do-	9-10-16	8 pm	The 10" Cheshires attacked at 12.35 took North face of STUFF REDOUBT & communication trenches up to points R21a.80, R21a.30, R21a.90. During attack we carried on overhead fire from Skyline Trench firing 20,000 rounds on barrage line along STUFF TRENCH & German front line running through R21a. As soon as line was taken & consolidated we moved two guns under Lieut Fay from South of the REDOUBT along east side up to points R21c.68 & R21c.38 men were in German dug outs. The enemy retaliated very heavily up to 7.30 pm. Visited tinspected positions at 10pm. Carrying out usual firing from Skyline & Schwaben on Grandcourt Rd. Enemy quiet. Sent back four guns from Skyline to transport. Guns damaged during the night (F.3117)	
-do-	10-10-16	2.45 pm	Continued consolidation of captured positions in STUFF REDOUBT the enemy were fairly quiet during the forenoon.	
-do-	11.10.16		But at 3 pm heavily shelled our trenches. Had 3 casualties.	
-do-	12-10-16		During forenoon enemy very quiet but started sudden bursts of Rear shelling in afternoon. During the evening I carried out a small attack which was easily repulsed, on STUFF REDOUBT.	

T2134. Wt. W708—776. 500000. 4/15. Sir J. C. & S.

Army Form C. 2118.

WAR DIARY
or
INTELLIGENCE SUMMARY.
(Erase heading not required.)

Instructions regarding War Diaries and Intelligence Summaries are contained in F. S. Regs., Part II. and the Staff Manual respectively. Title pages will be prepared in manuscript.

Place	Date	Hour	Summary of Events and Information	Remarks and references to Appendices
X23 Central	13-14		Carried out inter-section relief. N°4 going to front line, N°3 to support, N°1 to SKYLINE TRENCH, & N°2 to transport field. Connecting up of ald gun broken, while carrying out Barrage fire.	
"	14-15th	7PM	6.C. 75 M.G. Coy. came up with view to taking over on 15th. At 2.46 PM the 8 L.N.L. attacked communicating trenches running NORTH from STUFF REDOUBT. We carried out overland fire a STUFF TRENCH & Bundle Rd. with 6 guns from SKYLINE TRENCH. The attack appears to have been very successful & large numbers of prisoners being brought down.	
W8, Central	15		Relieved by 75 M.G. Coy. Four guns were left attached to 75 M.G. Coy. Company returned to BOUZINCOURT & took over tents at W8a central.	
"	16		General clean up. The attached 4 guns returned to us.	
"	17		General training.	
"	18		3 guns went into the line and reported to 6.C. 75 M.G. Coy pending an attack.	
"	19		Very wet. Cleaning guns in tents and held union. 4 guns still under 6.C. 75 M.G. Coy.	

Army Form C. 2118.

WAR DIARY
or
INTELLIGENCE SUMMARY.
(Erase heading not required.)

Instructions regarding War Diaries and Intelligence Summaries are contained in F.S. Regs., Part II. and the Staff Manual respectively. Title pages will be prepared in manuscript.

Place	Date	Hour	Summary of Events and Information	Remarks and references to Appendices
N8a central	20		General training. Teams guns still in attached 75 M.S. Coy	
" "	21		General training. Team guns attached to 75 M.S. Coy took up posn in SKYLINE TRENCH to ainst in attack made by 25 Divsn on REGINA TRENCH.	
BOUZINCOURT	22		Moved into huts in BOUZINCOURT. Team guns lent to 75 M.S. Coy rejoined us.	
HERISSART	23		Marched to HERISSART with the rest of 7th Brigade, arrived in billets 12 noon.	
GEZAINCOURT	24		Marched to GEZAINCOURT with 7th Bde. Very wet marching, arrived in billets 12.50 p.m.	
CANDAS	25		General cleaning and tidying up. Resting as much as possible. Moved to Billets at CANDAS arriving at 5 p.m.	
"	26		Very wet. Lectures in billets.	
"	27		General cleaning and packing of limbers.	
"	28		Wet. General preparations for entraining on 29th Feb. 1916	
"	29		7 M.S. Coy entrained at DOULENS & detrained at BAILLEUL.	
"	30		Billets in lo BIZET.	

Sh. Lect M.G. Coy
C.O. 7 M.G. Coy

7th Inf. Bde.

25th Division

7th Bde. MACHINE GUN COY.,

NOVEMBER, 1916.

Army Form C. 2118.

WAR DIARY
or
INTELLIGENCE SUMMARY.

(Erase heading not required.)

7th M. Gun Co

Instructions regarding War Diaries and Intelligence Summaries are contained in F.S. Regs., Part II. and the Staff Manual respectively. Title pages will be prepared in manuscript.

Place	Date	Hour	Summary of Events and Information	Remarks and references to Appendices
LE BIZET	31-10-16		Cleaning guns and preparing for trenches.	
"	1-11-16		11 guns of 7 M.G. Coy. took over in the trenches from 20 M.G. Coy. 6 guns being in the left sector (from 30v 28 a 27 in the front line, a line running just NORTH of BORDER AVE to MAISON 1875 (v 2 6 c). 5 being in right sector (RIVER LYS C.16 b 74). There are no boundaries. H.Q. remains in LE BIZET.	Coy. Bosses — TEERT 28 s 4.4. C.16 b 30.
"	2-11-16		Situation quiet. Indirect fire being carried out.	* Following are the normal indirect tough
"	3-11-16		Situation normal.	
"	4-11-16		Right Section relieved by 5 guns from LE BIZET.	DUMP (s 6 a 02). Bridge (s 11 c 95).
"	5-11-16		5 guns moved to discharge gas but weather intervened.	L'OSA MOILLE (s 12 b 56)
"	6-11-16		Situation normal.	
"	7-11-16		It was proposed to discharge gas but weather became unsuitable. LEFT SECTN relieved by 6 guns from LE BIZET. Sections are doing 6 days in & 3 out.	C.16 (s 17a 45). PETITE HALLE FM
"	8-11-16		Situation normal. Wet weather.	Railway at J.C. v 39 a 55 b. Loop trench + X roads
"	9-11-16		Situation normal.	
"	10-11-16		It was proposed to discharge gas at 10 PM operations were cancelled. Right Section relieved by 5 guns from LE BIZET.	C.11 & 4.9. 9th

Army Form C. 2118.

WAR DIARY
or
INTELLIGENCE SUMMARY.
(Erase heading not required.)

Instructions regarding War Diaries and Intelligence Summaries are contained in F. S. Regs., Part II. and the Staff Manual respectively. Title pages will be prepared in manuscript.

Place	Date	Hour	Summary of Events and Information	Remarks and references to Appendices
LE BIZET	11-11-16		Situation Normal. Gas was discharged on 25 Div front. It commenced at 10 P.M. In that time carried out as usual, 4000 rds. h.g. fires	LAUNDRY Wood C.16.3590.
"	12-11-16		Situat Normal. Usual indirect fire carried out, 3,500 rds.	WEIS FARM C.5.a.2.6.
"	13-11-16		Situat Normal. Usual firing carried out 4,000 rds. Left Sect'n relieved by guns from LE BIZET.	BONT ROUGE
"	14-11-16		Situat Normal. Germans discharged gas on our left flank. Usual indirect firing 2000.	German Crailei D.29 a 5.2.
"	15-11-16		Situat Normal. Our Artillery bombarded enemy front line between 3.12 PM & 3.42 PM.	
"	16-11-16		Enemy Artillery active on PLOEGSTEERT WOOD. Situation Normal. Our Artillery did some firing during the night. Right Sect'n relieved by guns from LE BIZET. Usual indirect fire 4,500 rds.	
"	17-11-16		Situat Normal. Enemy Artillery active on PLOEGSTEERT WOOD. Usual firing 3000 rds.	
"	18-11-16		Situat Normal. Usual firing by M.G.S. 4750 rds.	
"	19-11-16		Situat Normal. Enemy shelled MAISON 1875 about mid-day. Left Sect'n relieved by guns from LE BIZET. Usual indirect firing carried out.	
	20-11-16		Situat. Normal. Usual indirect fire carried at 4500 rds.	
	21-11-16		Situat Normal. Little artillery activity on usual firing on indirect targets 3000 rds	

T2134. Wt. W708—776. 500000. 4/15. Sir J. C. & S.

Army Form C. 2118.

WAR DIARY
or
INTELLIGENCE SUMMARY.
(Erase heading not required.)

Instructions regarding War Diaries and Intelligence Summaries are contained in F. S. Regs., Part II. and the Staff Manual respectively. Title pages will be prepared in manuscript.

Place	Date	Hour	Summary of Events and Information	Remarks and references to Appendices
LE BIZET	22-4-16		Situation normal. Some Trench mortar activity on both sides in Right Sector. Right Sector relieved by guns from LE BIZET. Usual indirect firing. 400 rds	
"	23-4-16		Situation normal. 1708 fired from 1st V Wks (8) 10E CHESHIRE (4) Firing kept up on increased establishment. S00 16 to open up. Usual firing.	
"	24-4-16		Situation Normal. Usual firing on indirect targets	
"	25-4-16		Situation normal. Enemy Artillery slightly active during the night 24/25. Left Sector relieved by guns from LE BIZET. Usual indirect fire 5000.	
"	26-4-16		Situation normal. Church parade for m.g. at trenches. Usual firing on indirect Targets.	
"	27-4-16		Situation Normal. Enemy Artillery registered throughout the morning on both Sectors. Indirect fire carried out as usual. Guns inspected by Div. General.	
"	28-4-16		Situation normal. Enemy Artillery slight, active all day. Enemy T.M.B also active near BARKENHAM Farm. Usual firing on indirect Targets. 5000 rds.	

D. Lee M. M. F Capt.
7 M.G. Coy

7th Inf. Bde.

25th Division

7th Bde. MACHINE GUN COY.,

DECEMBER, 1916.

Army Form C. 2118.

Vol 1 Z
7. Machine Gun Coy

WAR DIARY
or
INTELLIGENCE SUMMARY.
(Erase heading not required.)

Instructions regarding War Diaries and Intelligence Summaries are contained in F. S. Regs., Part II. and the Staff Manual respectively. Title pages will be prepared in manuscript.

Place	Date	Hour	Summary of Events and Information	Remarks and references to Appendices
LE BIZET	29-11-16		Situation Normal. Enemy TMB & artillery active during the morning. Our Artillery also active. Usual indirect fire carried out 6000 rounds.	
"	30-11-16		Situation Normal. Enemy TMB active between 2PM & 4PM on right sector. Usual indirect fire carried out 5000 rds	
"	1-12-16		Situation Normal. Quiet. Left Sector relieved by guns from LE BIZET. Our MG fired an usual indirect Targets 6000 rds	
	2-12-16		Situation Normal. Artillery on both sides slightly active. Usual indirect fire carried out.	
	3-12-16		Situation Normal. Germans a gas alarm our Sphere. Usual firing carried out.	
	4-12-16		Situation Normal. Right Sector relieved by guns from LE BIZET. Our Artillery slightly active. Enemy TMB active Aft Sector. Usual firing carried out.	
	5-12-16		Situation Normal. There was two gas alarms at 5.15 PM. and 11PM. No damage done. Usual firing carried out on Indirect Targets. Our artillery fairly active.	
	6-12-16		Three guns CHESHIRE PLOEGSTEERT and COVENT were relieved by 3 guns of 75th B.de. The morning Our left sectors night Trench is run SUFFOLK AVE. & our 3 guns have returned to LE BIZET. There are now 9 guns in use. CARTER'S FM. BARKENHAM, H.Q. FM Anti-aircraft, NAPOO and SCREEN. (These are all I sector)	

WAR DIARY
or
INTELLIGENCE SUMMARY

Army Form C. 2118.

Place	Date	Hour	Summary of Events and Information	Remarks and references to Appendices
LE BIZET	6-12-16		RESERVE F⁰ NICHOLSON and VILLOWS (Left Sectr). S.Tract: Normal, quiet day. Usual indirect fire carried out by right sectr.	
"	7-12-16		N⁰ 2 Section took over the following positions Villows Reserve F⁰ Nicholson SCREEN. N⁰ 3 Section took over the following positions. LYS F⁰ (One is a new position on extreme right of Brigade Sectr) Anti-aircraft, H & F⁰ & NAPOO. Two Guns of N⁰ 1 Sectr over BARTENHAM & CARTERS. (One F⁰ & one gun are to be relieved every 2 days.) N⁰ 2 sectr 2 teams & N⁰ 1 remain in billets. Indirect fire carried out as usual quiet day and frequent billet are now on follows. N⁰ 1 sectn. Mr. Jenner & Mr. Brownlow N⁰ 2 sectr Mr. Powell & Lt. Smith. N⁰ 3 Lt Lang & 2/Lt Leth. H.Q. Sect: 2/Lt Hutchison. Transport etc at Bac-St-Nieppe under Lt Williamson.	
	8-12-16		Sitn at: Normal. Usual indirect fire carried out by SCREEN, H & F⁰ & NAPOO guns. Left sectr relieved.	
	9-12-16		S.Tract: Normal. Guns in Villows point Rt Butter(?)(Bangh) barrel casing, usual indirect fire by SCREEN, NAPOO TH.& F⁰ guns. Enemy TM's active in Left sectr near NICKOLSON gun.	
	10-12-16		Situation: Normal. Enemy Artillery slightly active, usual indirect fire. Usual Barrage fr.	

WAR DIARY
or
INTELLIGENCE SUMMARY.
(Erase heading not required.)

Army Form C. 2118.

Place	Date	Hour	Summary of Events and Information	Remarks and references to Appendices
LE BRET	10-12-16		Relief of trenches	
	11-12-16		At 12:20AM 1/4 KRRC Rgt Gun Artillery active on right of our sector. Enemy shelled ARMENTIERES, right to left. In relieved by guns from LE BRET. Artillery & Trench Mortars quiet. Situation normal. Usual trench & mid-fire carried out.	
	12-12-16		Situation Normal. Usual indirect fire carried out. Artillery quiet. Also T.M.B.	
	13-12-16		Situation Normal. Slight artillery activity on both sides. Enemy 18 pounders fired some shells on to Support Line. Indirect fire was carried out & SCREEN & WILLOWS GUN Well being continued on officers dug out, right sector and on M.G. Emplacement in RENT AVE. Reinforcements to complete establishments arrived as follows. 8 L.N.LANCS. 8 men. 3rd WORCESTER 8 men.	
	14-12-16		Situation Normal. Our Artillery slightly active during the forenoon. Our Artillery fired intermittently from 5PM – 8PM on enemy Trench tramway and transport routes. T.M.B.s quiet. Indirect fire carried out by H&F.B – CARTER'S gun.	
	15-12-16		Situation Normal. Enemy Machine Guns fired at right of our line normal in Reserve F.S. Artillery quiet. Our M.G. active firing on enemy road and communication Trenches also indirect targets by day. Our Artillery carried out wire cutting as yet not completed.	

WAR DIARY
or
INTELLIGENCE SUMMARY

Army Form C. 2118.

Place	Date	Hour	Summary of Events and Information	Remarks and references to Appendices
LE BIZET	16.12.16		Situat: normal. Gun Artillery carried on wire cutting during daylight. Gun Machine guns fired on enemy gaps & enemy wire during night 16/17 Initial. Normal firing on indirect targets by day. Will be carried on an indirect fire policy at H & F.B. 3rd rgt at LETOUQUET STATN. Enfilact L. KENT road to be worked at G. RES. SCREEN indirect fire enfilact road. Finished. Enemy Artillery quiet. Also TMBs.	
	17.12.16		Situat: Normal. Right Sectn relieved by teams from LE BIZET. Enemy Artillery & Gun Artillery quiet. Enemy TMBs quiet. Enemy M.G. slightly active at night, not on any particular target. Our M.G fired on usual indirect targets. Average daily expenditure of ammunt 5000 rds. 3 reinforcements arrived from base. Situat: Normal. We received 3 limber G.S. Waggons in place of 3 S.A.A. Carts. Artillery & TMBs quiet. Normal indirect firing. There was a Brigade relief for Co's at 11 A.M. prior to Brittal relief. We'd arr to take place on 15th inst. Normal work being carried on as usual. Enemy during [unreadable] also saw indirect fire policy. General [unreadable] in direct front.	
	18.12.16			
	19.12.16		Situat: Normal. Gun Artillery slightly active on enemy mortar handles between 2.10 P.M. - 4 P.M.	

WAR DIARY or INTELLIGENCE SUMMARY

Army Form C. 2118.

Place	Date	Hour	Summary of Events and Information	Remarks and references to Appendices
LE BIZET	19-12-16		Enemy TM Bs & MGs quiet. Enemy MGs fire burst during night & fired a RESERVE FM & Road between it and DES PIERRIES. Gun M.G. fired on wired indirect Target both by day & night. Work on MG posns. Digging away part of trench falls in at WILLOWS Gun. Driving concrete influence WILLOWS Gun roofs made G for alternative post at SCREEN Gun. Clean wet dug-outs & stores at RESERVE FM.	
	20-12-16		Situation Normal. Enemy Artillery quiet. Gun Artillery active about 3.45pm. Enemy TMs active about 20 shells. Enemy M.G. quiet. Own M.G. carried out indirect fire on SCREEN, NAPOO H.Q. & RESERVE FM. Work driving trenches around emplacements. Turning indirect fire positions at SCREEN H.Q. & RESERVE FM. There was a meeting of officers at 11am at LE TOUQUET STATION. Left Sector relieved by Guns from LE BIZET.	
	21-12-16		Situation Normal. Gun Artillery fired intermittently all day. Enemy artillery quiet. Enemy TMBs fired a little in Left Sector. Own retaliated. M.G. Enemy quiet. Own M.G. fired on usual indirect Targets. Work done repairing head around NICHOLSON Gun, also work in Emplacements. Enemy Sanded was Bombarded by Artillery.	
	22-12-16		Situation normal. Usual firing on indirect targets. Quite.	
	23-12-16		Situation normal. There was an officers' meeting at right sector H.Q. at 11am. Artillery activity slight. Enemy M.G.s slightly active during night 22/23. Usual firing	

Army Form C. 2118.

WAR DIARY
or
INTELLIGENCE SUMMARY.
(Erase heading not required.)

Instructions regarding War Diaries and Intelligence Summaries are contained in F. S. Regs., Part II. and the Staff Manual respectively. Title pages will be prepared in manuscript.

Place	Date	Hour	Summary of Events and Information	Remarks and references to Appendices
LE BIZET	23.12.16		On indirect targets by day and night. It was carried out by Lys 1st gun. Shots officer lay shots up to the front line across our Rgt & opposed effect. Right Section relieved by guns from Pn.	
"	24.12.16		Situat normal. Arrangements made for known dumps of me ant of trenches. Ranged M.G. firing on indirect targets. Unit being carried on at Transport field and on emplacement of the line. Couldn't provide for me out of trench.	
	25.12.16		Situat normal. Our M.G. more active. Enemy would 5000 rds in all by fired. Brigade on our left carried out a raid. Our front line left of D. Coy. was bombarded & retaliated during the raid. No casualties. Known dumps provided for men out of trenches. Enemy quiet.	
	26.12.16		Right Sectn relieved by guns from LE BIZET. Situat normal. Would indirect fire carried out. Enemy M.G's delt acting at night firing on road running from LE TOUQUET Stn & road from DESPIERRE Fm.	
	27.12.16		Situat normal. Enemy artill quiet also ours, Enemy & our TM B's quiet. Enemy M.G. fired occasional bursts during the night. No definite target. Our M.G. fired as usual. Usual CT for H.Q F.M. alternative Emplacement. New return fire H.Q F.M. gun. New dug-out at	

Army Form C. 2118.

WAR DIARY
or
INTELLIGENCE SUMMARY.
(Erase heading not required.)

Instructions regarding War Diaries and Intelligence Summaries are contained in F. S. Regs., Part II. and the Staff Manual respectively. Title pages will be prepared in manuscript.

Place	Date	Hour	Summary of Events and Information	Remarks and references to Appendices
LE BIZET	27-12-16		M.G. H.Q. right section.	
	28-12-16		Situation normal. Our artillery slightly active on our right. Usual indirect fire carried out by our M.G. Enemy quiet. Work being carried out as yesterday.	
			During the month we have fired approximately 103,870 rounds on indirect targets which are as follows :—	
			Road Bridge C5d 70,25. Brewery & Vat E17a 3:7. L'OSA MOELLE C12 b 56.	
			X roads C11 c 80 60 Junct. of Trench & road C6d 54,35 C.T. D29 a 37.	
			Road C6b 30,20 to C12 b 65,10. Jnct. Ring & C29 b 34,90. Trench Junct. D22 b 99.	
			DURIEZ F.M. C5A 20. X rds D30 c 15,15 Bridge C5a 35,50	
			Sunken Bridge & CT C11a 50,15 NECKLACE C.T. C11b 50,10 Track C11 b 95,05	
			C.T. running S.W. of White Farm C5a 20,60. Bridge C11a 45,15. CT. at C11a 50,15	
			Junct. C6a 0.2. Chicken Run C11a 45. Rd. D23 c 60,35	
			X rds C11 b C12 b 95,00 X rds C11c 95,00 & Earle Rouge.	
			Iron Bridge C11 b 4.9. X rds C11 b 90.40 Jnct. of track C6 b 6 24	

B.R. Lee M.M.
T.M.G.C.y

WAR DIARY
INTELLIGENCE SUMMARY

7 M G Coy   Vol /3   Army Form C. 2118.

Place	Date	Hour	Summary of Events and Information	Remarks and references to Appendices
LE BIZET	29-12-16		Situat. Normal. Our Artillery fired on Enemy Wire & front line. Enemy Artillery quiet. Our TMB fired on Wire. Enemy retaliated on left of BARKENHAM Row. Enemy M.G. was active during night. 29/30. Our M.G. fired usual targets. Also on our 4 gaps in the wire. Work to carried on an Anti-aircraft front line Reserve Arm. 2 wnty wds from dug out at H.Q. F.S. Right sect. relieved by LE BIZET.	
"	30-12-16		Situat. normal. Enemy Artillery put some shells into Batt H.Q. right sector. About 50 shells in all. Our Artillery was active. Our usual 6 LE TOUQUET sect. Our M.G. fired on usual Targets. Work to carried on an Anti-aircraft front near Reserve Farm.	
"	31-12-16		Situat. Normal. G.C. conference at Brigade H.Q. at 10.30 AM. Enemy Artillery slightly active about mid-day. Our Artillery fired active during the morning. Our M.G. fired as usual. Work still in progress on Anti-aircraft post at Reserve Fm	
"	1-1-17		Artillery shelled enemy wire and front line defences in front of left sector. from 10.30 AM onwards. Divisional Major M.G. Coy, was round the right sect. today. Our M.G. fired Barrages the night ½ hr on gaps in enemy wire.	

WAR DIARY
or
INTELLIGENCE SUMMARY.
(Erase heading not required.)

Army Form C. 2118.

Place	Date	Hour	Summary of Events and Information	Remarks and references to Appendices
LE BIZET	1-1-17		195th Coy. Placed 5 guns under our control, 4 rear guns took up positions at Cecilia AVENUE, LANCASHIRE Sap at F5. BURNT OUT F6 CONVENT GUN, & DUDLEY FORT. The Bde extended before the left boundary is now BORDER AVE.	
"	2-1-17		Enemy quiet. Situation normal. Turned M.G. Officer with a gun round the trenches. Re Gun condemned BURNT OUT F5 & DUDLEY FORT & CARTERS Gun positions. Usual indirect fire carried out, & work still in progress.	
"	3-1-17		Enemy quiet, Situation normal, Conf. M.G. Officers was here. Usual Indirect fire barrages & work proceeding satisfactorily	
"	4-1-17		Enemy quiet. Our Artillery Bombarded Enemy Lines in front of 6 Corps. Enemy retaliated with H.E. Rounds RESERVE & GUNNERS FARM. Several Gas shells were thrown over the D.M.G.O. was round & went up the line to right Sect/7 new positions selected for Carters FARM GUN in LONG AVE. Usual indirect fire carried out & work still in progress.	
"	5-1-17		Enemy quiet. Situation normal. Permission was granted by Brigade to move the following Guns 15 New positions selected by D.M. Boffen. Willows Gun, Carters Gun. BURNT OUT FARM CONVENT GUN, DUDLEY FORT, Antitank craft positions were	

Army Form C. 2118.

WAR DIARY
or
INTELLIGENCE SUMMARY.
(Erase heading not required.)

Instructions regarding War Diaries and Intelligence Summaries are contained in F. S. Regs., Part II. and the Staff Manual respectively. Title pages will be prepared in manuscript.

Place	Date	Hour	Summary of Events and Information	Remarks and references to Appendices
LE BIZET	5.1.17		were buried at LANCASHIRE SUPPORT FARM, RESERVE FARM, PLOEGSTEERT WOOD. All platforms & positions were subject to direct and indirect fire but Concrete. The usual indirect fire was carried out. Work still in progress.	
"	6.1.17		Enemy Artillery slightly active, but Artillery active in Le TOUQUET SECTOR. Usual indirect fire was carried out. Work still in progress.	
"	7.1.17		Situation normal. Enemy quiet. Reliefs took place. Y noml indirect fire work 5th Hy Pynrs.	
"	8.1.17		Situation normal. Enemy quiet, a bombardment took place on our left of the Enemy's defences. Indirect fire as normal. Work still in progress.	
"	9.1.17		Our Artillery bombarded Enemy's defence line in front of Hill 63, Y PLOEGSTEERT WOOD. Enemy replies by shelling the Wood, D.M.G. areas & gun teams. Y Keel positions were chosen for a Reserve line in case of a attack on the following ANNE PEGENTREES ANE, PAMPADOUR FARM, LONDON FARM, Y PLOEGSTEERT WOOD position. A new defence scheme is being the Condemned RESERVE FARM position. A new defence scheme is being drawn up by Lny line.	
"	10.1.17		Situation normal. Enemy moderately active on both sectors. Bombardment beyond	

T2134. Wt. W708—776. 500000. 4/15. Sr J. C. & S.

WAR DIARY
or
INTELLIGENCE SUMMARY.

Army Form C. 2118.

Place	Date	Hour	Summary of Events and Information	Remarks and references to Appendices
LE BIZET	10.1.17		Artillery & TM'B° of Enemy Defences knoll, new positions were occupied by our Gun teams at POMPADOUR FARM, SEVENTREES AVE CULVERT GUN, KENT AVE. Work is progressing Data factory at all these positions, in dug out & Emplacement	
"	11.1.17		Situation normal, Enemy Artillery bombarded our front line in B Coy. Work still in progress at all new Gun positions.	
"	12.1.17		D.M.G. Officer was here & enquired about new positions & progress of work, he afterwards went round the line was quite satisfied. RESERVE FARM position was taken over by 195th M.G. Coy teams, which are under our control. Situation normal. Enemy Very quiet.	
"	13.1.17		Situation normal, Enemy quiet, Construction of new positions & work in general progressing very favorably. No firing took place owing to night work being in progress.	
"	14.1.17		Situation Normal, Enemy Artillery fired a few rounds were exclusively laying on LE TOUQUET STN. D.M. Gun Officer was round & went up the line, Work is proceeding very satisfactorily, he has continued Kent Ave. position.	

Army Form C. 2118.

WAR DIARY
or
INTELLIGENCE SUMMARY.
(Erase heading not required.)

Instructions regarding War Diaries and Intelligence Summaries are contained in F. S. Regs., Part II. and the Staff Manual respectively. Title pages will be prepared in manuscript.

Place	Date	Hour	Summary of Events and Information	Remarks and references to Appendices
LE BIZET	14.1.17		Firing took placed normally. Very misty, snow & frost at night.	
"	15.1.17		Situation normal. Enemy quiet. Went to inspect new camp at Carters B.C. 75th Scary Officers went round the line junior to taking over sections. Work still in progress.	
"	16.1.17		Situation normal. Enemy slightly active. New Lewis guns arrived in LE BIZET tomorrow 16. Work still in progress 800.	
"	17.1.17		Taking over line, Guns were taken up the line. Work still in progress. Moves out of LE BIZET to new camp at Carter's camp.	
CARTERS CAMP	18.1.17		Training in mechanism & stoppages & in the Barr & Stroud Range Finder. Gun drill in the afternoon. Lecture on range cards on the attack & defence.	
"	19.1.17		Physical training, cleaning gun. Sphere parts etc. Training in mechanism & stoppages. The company (minus) for baths in the afternoon.	
"	20.1.17		Physical training, training in mechanism & stoppages. Lieut L. Thrashie joins the Company as 2 in Command.	
"	21.1.17		Church Parade with 1st Wilts Regt.	
"	22.1.17		Route march & tactical exercise. The sections had orders to take up a position along the defensive line. The position taken up by each gun, & the orders issued etc. were then criticised by the C.O.	

Army Form C. 2118.

WAR DIARY
or
INTELLIGENCE SUMMARY.
(Erase heading not required.)

Instructions regarding War Diaries and Intelligence Summaries are contained in F. S. Regs., Part II. and the Staff Manual respectively. Title pages will be prepared in manuscript.

Place	Date	Hour	Summary of Events and Information	Remarks and references to Appendices
CARTER'S CAMP	23.1.17		The Company leaves CARTER'S CAMP & moves into camp in ROMERIN [T26d42]. Lecture in the afternoon on Characteristics of the machine gun.	
"	24.1.17		Physical training. Range Practice. Games in afternoon & lecture.	
"	25.1.17		Lecture and practical demonstration by Brigade Shooting Officer. The C.O. and three officers visit the Kemmel defences. Visit from the Corps Machine Gun Officer. Through chewing of gun. In the afternoon the Company played Football.	
	26.1.17		Physical training. Advanced drill, range finding and range cards. Tactical Scheme in which the Company took up a defensive position along a railway. The Special attention being paid to inter-communication and orders. Football in the afternoon. The C.O. & three officers reconnoitre a second line of defence. Lecture in the evening on Parts. Table C. C.O. gave lecture to 10th Cheshires on M.Gs.	

J. Douglas Marks, Major
Commanding 9. (Ch)
T.134. Wt. W708—776. 500000. 4/15. Sir J. C. & S.

Staff Capt
7 Inf Bde

Herewith original copy War Diary of this Unit from 27-1-17 to 27-2-17

                                    for MAJOR,
                    COMDG. 7th MACHINE GUN COY.

No. 7
MACHINE GUN
COMPANY.
No. AD 28
Date 27-2-17

WAR DIARY or INTELLIGENCE SUMMARY

Army Form C. 2118.

7 M G Coy

Vol 14

Place	Date	Hour	Summary of Events and Information	Remarks and references to Appendices
CAMP T26 d.4.2 R.5 Map 28 S.W3 1/10000	27.1.16		The morning and part of the afternoon was spent at the range firing Guns & Table C. Also the men were practised in firing with their Steel Helmets on and with the Emerg(enc)y Exp(osure). The remainder of the day spent in cleaning guns. Lecture in the evening on "Overhead Fire"	
	28.1.16		Church Parade with 1st Wilts Regt in morning. Equipment scrubbed and polished in the afternoon. The C.O. and section officers reconnoitre the part of the line to be taken over by us.	
	29.1.16		Stoppages and mechanism during the morning. A talk on the care and attention to be given to Stoppages. Guns and equipment cleaned during the afternoon. In the evening lecture on "Indirect Fire on attack", followed by concert in Company canteen.	
	30.1.16		Physical Training in the morning followed by Tactical scheme, the chief points of which were Ammunition Supply, and overhead fire. Eight Guns Web(?) of defensive fire. Exhibit the regiments eight put up a Barrage by employing indirect Overhead fire. Gun cleaning in the afternoon. 2 Lt Hay rejoins the Company from Hospital.	

Army Form C. 2118.

WAR DIARY
or
INTELLIGENCE SUMMARY.
(Erase heading not required.)

Instructions regarding War Diaries and Intelligence Summaries are contained in F.S. Regs., Part II. and the Staff Manual respectively. Title pages will be prepared in manuscript.

Place	Date	Hour	Summary of Events and Information	Remarks and references to Appendices
CAMP T26L4.2 Res.M.G 28.S.W.3.1/10000	31.1.17		Overhauling guns, stores, kits, etc. The Company march to PONT NIEPPE for bath on their way back the change dispatch box respirator at the Guy's Gas School. The C.O. visits 74 M.G. Coy. to make arrangements about the relief. In the afternoon the C.O. inspects the Coy. in full marching order and afterwards holds a kit inspection.	
"	1.2.17		Preparing for the trenches. In the afternoon the Coy. moves up into Reserve Billets in PLOEGSTEERT WOOD and takes over the Reserve gun position from 74th M.G. Coy. The C.O. attends a Commanding Officer's Conference in the evening.	
PLOEGSTEERT SECTOR	2.2.17		Nos 1 and 2 Sections relieve the advanced guns of 74 M.G. Coy. The C.O's of both Coy's visit the guns just after the relief. During the day we fired 2000 rounds Indirect fire from MUD LANE I.T. position. Day passed quietly.	
	3.2.17		The day and night passed quietly but there was unusual battle aerial activity. One of our gun fired on an enemy aeroplane which crossed our lines. Major Drummond, D.S.O. Brigade Gun Officer visited our position. We carried out 2000 Rds. Indirect fire on enemy Communication trenches.	
	4.2.17		Slight hostile trench mortar activity at intervals to which our trench mortars replied. Our Machine Guns fired 1000 rounds Indirect fire on enemy C.T's and tracks. The C.O. held a conference of officers at	

T2134. Wt. W708½ 776. 600,000. 2/15/59. Sir J. C. & S.

Army Form C. 2118.

WAR DIARY
or
INTELLIGENCE SUMMARY.
(Erase heading not required.)

Place	Date	Hour	Summary of Events and Information	Remarks and references to Appendices
PLOEGSTEERT SECTOR	5.2.17		Nos. 3 and 4 Section relieved Nos. 1 and 2 in the forward position during the morning. During the afternoon our artillery, machine guns and trench mortars carried out a bombardment of the enemy lines. Our machine guns carried out barrage fire on enemy C.T.'s. 8,500 rounds were fired. The C.O. visited the gun during the morning and checked the ranges, elevation etc. In the evening the C.O. attended a Commanding Officers Conference at Brigade Headquarters.	
	6.2.17		Slight reciprocal trench mortar activity, otherwise the day passed very quietly. We carried out indirect fire on enemy communication trenches. The C.O. visited the transport lines then moving the Section in reserve we carried out improvements to Reserve Billets, the work is much delayed by the difficulty in getting material.	
	7.2.17		Enemy fairly active with trench mortars. Artillery of both sides quiet. Our machine gun carried out the usual indirect fire on enemy C.T.'s and roads and fired 3,250 rounds. Enemy machine guns were very quiet. We carried at work on improvements to the gun positions and also to Reserve Billets.	
	8.2.17		Nos. 1 & 2 Section relieved Nos. 3 & 4 in the forward position during the morning. There was considerable hostile trench mortar activity during the morning. Hostile aeroplanes were active and were engaged by our anti-aircraft guns.	

Army Form C. 2118.

WAR DIARY
or
INTELLIGENCE SUMMARY.
(Erase heading not required.)

Place	Date	Hour	Summary of Events and Information	Remarks and references to Appendices
PLOEGSTEERT SECTOR	9.2.17		We carried out a few bursts of fire into the enemies lines with artillery and trench mortars. The enemy retaliated but did not do any considerable damage. We carried out our usual indirect fire on enemy C.T.'s & tracks and also engaged three hostile aeroplanes. Work is progressing on dugout & improvement to position & Reserve Billets. The C.O. attended a conference at Brigade H.Q.	
	10.2.17		After Rickman joined the coy from the base. Things quiet but the usual aerial activity on both sides. Our anti-aircraft gun engaged several hostile aeroplanes and fired 700 rounds. The usual indirect fire was carried out during the night. Work is progress on a new dugout in the line and a improvement to Gun Position. The C.O. held a meeting of all officers during the morning.	
	11.2.17		Our gun on St Yves Hill got shelled for a short period during the morning but no damage was done. The C.O. and Major Emmond, Divie R.S.O., visited the gun in the Right Sector this morning. Church parade is Reserve Hut this afternoon. The C.O. visited the transport lines this afternoon. A package containing a German fork and German field postcards was found by one of our men in the wood this afternoon.	
	12.2.17		The day & night passed fairly quietly with the exception of the T.M.'s on Right Sector this afternoon. The C.O. and the Brigade Major went round the position this morning. Work is progressing satisfactorily on the dugout. Thirteen overhead gun positions are being prepared in view of a coming raid. The weather is turning warmer.	

T2134. Wt. W708—776. 500000. 4/15. Sir J. C. & S.

WAR DIARY or INTELLIGENCE SUMMARY

Army Form C. 2118.

Place	Date	Hour	Summary of Events and Information	Remarks and references to Appendices
PLOEGSTEERT SECTOR	13.2.17		A fine bright day. Our artillery and trench mortars have been cutting wire throughout the day. We have completed the thirteen machine gun defended fire positions which we started yesterday. Work still in progress in the dugout. Working parties in sent up to assist during the day from Reserve Billets. There was a re-arrangement of all officers this morning.	
	14.2.17		Our Artillery and French mortars have again been wire cutting to-day. Hostile Artillery was somewhat active this evening. Numbers 192 Section relieved numbers 39 & this morning. The latter return this afternoon. The enemy and a new Star shell last night of unusual brilliance. We had one man killed this evening (Pte. Pincher) while returning from fetching rations.	
	15.2.17		Our artillery and trench mortars have been active to-day. The enemy for only retaliated slightly. We carried out our usual indirect fire during the night, and at midday to-day (we fire) as the enemy first line during an artillery wire cutting bombardment. Funeral of Pte. Pincher during morning.	
	16.2.17		Artillery active on our front but not much retaliation. We placed out our Lewis Gun to-day. In to-morrow overhead fire. The O.C. lectured the men Lewis Guns & O.R. to-morrow and on Enemy Machine Guns.	

Place	Date	Hour	Summary of Events and Information	Remarks and references to Appendices
PLOEGSTEERT SECTOR Ref. Trench Map 28 S.W.4 1/10000	17.2.17		The 7th Brigade carried out a daylight raid this morning on enemy's front & support trenches in which machine gun cooperated. O.C. 7th M.G.Coy submitted to Brigade a scheme of cooperation which was adhered to in subsequent operation orders. Eight guns, teams, etc were detailed from 75th Machine Gun Coy and two from 1/5 Coy. Guns were allocated as follows. Two guns in front line to carry out flank shooting in support front across with direct fire on the left flank of the enemy. Seven guns in battle position on St Yves hill and ground in vicinity were detailed to fire on enemy strongholds & open in the open, owing to the quantity of smoke however nothing could be seen. Fifteen guns on the other side being employed on a German communication, support, & reserve trenches. The infantry taking part in the raid stated that considerable help was given them both by the guns on the flanks & also the guns doing indirect fire	*U14 C 85.10 – U14 C 8.3

WAR DIARY or INTELLIGENCE SUMMARY.

Army Form C. 2118.

Place	Date	Hour	Summary of Events and Information	Remarks and references to Appendices
PLOEGSTEERT SECTOR	18.2.17		The night and day passed quietly. In the morning the C.O. visited the guns in the line after the sections had carried out the inter-section relief of Church Parade was held in the afternoon at Reserve Billets. We carried out our usual indirect fire from MUD LANE position.	
	19.2.17		A fair & quiet day with slight reciprocal artillery activity. The C.O. visited the guns on the line during the morning. The new dugout at ANNSCROFT position has been practically completed.	
	20.2.17		The weather has turned very misty & in consequence of the bad visibility there is very little artillery activity. The C.O. visited the guns in the line during the morning to make arrangements for the relief. Punctified by Brigade tonight the relief commences tomorrow.	
	21.2.17		Nos 1, 2, 4 section relieved by section of 3rd New Zealand Machine Gun Coy. (M) Withdrawn to camp near ROMARIN. 2nd M. Coy arrange billets in PIERROUCK for the company	
	22.2.17		No 3 Section relieved as St Yves Hill and withdrawn to camp where it rejoins rest of coy. & remains for the night.	

WAR DIARY or INTELLIGENCE SUMMARY

Army Form C. 2118.

Place	Date	Hour	Summary of Events and Information	Remarks and references to Appendices
CAMP T26d42 Ref Maps 28 S.W.S.Ypres	23.2.17		The Coy. leaves Camp and marches to PIEBROUCK via BAILLEUL. Br. Bulford, the Brigadier watched the Brigade march past. Destination reached by about 2 P.M. Billets very rough (sic), the men in barns. The horse lines have much standing but no shelter from the weather.	
PIEBROUCK	24.2.17		The morning was spent cleaning up and cleaning gun equipment etc also clearing stable yards. Five men sent down to the Base, the medically unfit and four for transfer to the infantry in being unsuitable for machine gunners. A lot of deficiencies in gun equipment were made out during the morning. R.C. service in Berthen Church at 11 A.M. Church parade for Coy. C of E. in the afternoon. Billets.	
	25.2.17		Lieut Jesson and a Lance Corporal proceed to CAMIERS for a course of machine gun instruction. Cleaning up and scrubbing equipment in the morning. In the afternoon there was a football match between 1 and 2 section v. 3 and 4 section v. Officers and grooms riding class in the evening.	
	26.2.17			

[signature]
for MAJOR,
O.O.M.D.G. 7th MACHINE GUN COY.

Army Form C. 2118.

4th Machine Gun Coy

Vol 15

WAR DIARY or INTELLIGENCE SUMMARY.
(Erase heading not required.)

Place	Date	Hour	Summary of Events and Information	Remarks and references to Appendices
PIEBROUCK	27.2.17		The section were at the disposal of section officers during the morning. The time was chiefly spent in through overhaul of guns, making up deficiencies in kit and general clean up. The afternoon there was a cross country run for the whole company. Small prizes being given to the first three to finish.	
	28.2.17		The morning was spent at hecksam and stoppages and machine gun drill. In the afternoon the opening matches of a football tournament were played. Headquarters played No. 4 sect. & won, and the Transport won their match against No. 1 Sect. The men showed considerable enthusiasm in the games.	
	1.3.17		In the morning the whole company was out through gunning practice on a 25 yards range and afterwards revolver practice was carried out. In the afternoon the O.C. proceeded to the Worcestan Headquarters to attend a gas demonstration. The Glosters there arrived very late consequently the demonstration was cancelled. Ruling & jumping clases in the evening for officers & grooms.	
	2.3.17		Route march and tactical scheme in the morning. The guns were brought into action with a view to defending the Line of R. Road. Up soon on the guns were in position. The C.O. visited them and criticised the ammunition supply, intercommunication and orders. The same kind of the inter section matches was played this afternoon. H.Q. beat the Transport, and No. 2 & 3 section drew.	

WAR DIARY or INTELLIGENCE SUMMARY

Army Form C. 2118.

Place	Date	Hour	Summary of Events and Information	Remarks and references to Appendices
PIEBROUCK	3.3.17		The usual Physical Training before breakfast. Probationers, Stretcher bearers and Signallers drill during the morning. Inter-section cross country race in the afternoon, won by Coy. H.Q. section. C.O. attends Conference in the evening. Company turn out.	
"	4.3.17		Articles of Kit issued to Headquarters, Transport, No.s 3 & 4 sections in the morning. Church Parade at 11 A.M. followed by riding class. Football match between Nos. 2 & 3 sections in afternoon resulting in won for No. 2	
	5.3.17		Stoppages carried out in the billets and kit issued to the remainder of the Company. Lecture for officers & N.C.O's on Bayonet fighting by Captain Betts. Football match in the afternoon between N.C.O's held resulting in won for N.C.O's.	
	6.3.17		Gas Demonstration with the 3rd Worcester Regt. Practice in adjusting the respirators whilst advancing first through Stoke bomb and then through cloud gas. Remainder of the morning Squad drill and machine gun drill. Football match between H.Q. and No.2 sect. resulting in won for No. 2.	

Army Form C. 2118.

WAR DIARY
or
INTELLIGENCE SUMMARY.
(Erase heading not required.)

Instructions regarding War Diaries and Intelligence Summaries are contained in F. S. Regs., Part II. and the Staff Manual respectively. Title pages will be prepared in manuscript.

Place	Date	Hour	Summary of Events and Information	Remarks and references to Appendices
PIEBROUCK	7.3.17		Physical training, gun cleaning, bayonet drill and revolver practice in the morning. Football match in the afternoon against the 10th Cheshires who were left a goal game. Cinema concert with the 10th Cheshires was given after the game. The Corps M.S.O. visited the company today.	
	8.3.17		Physical training, gun cleaning and range finding during the morning. Section Officers and C.O. held conference in tent etc. The C.O. visited D.A.D.O.S. in the afternoon to hasten the supply of certain articles of equipment which had been indented for.	
	9.3.17		Brigade route march of about 16 miles. No.1 Section was detailed to form part of the advanced guard. They carried their gun equipment etc. on pack animals. The S.O.C. Brigade appeared pleased with the turn out of the company.	
	10.3.17		Sections at the disposal of Section Officers during the morning. Limbers fitted with leather tops for carrying filling ones etc. A football match Officers v Sergeants took place in the afternoon resulting in win for Sergeants.	

T.2131. Wt. W708-776. 500000. 4/15. Sir J. C. & S.

WAR DIARY
or
INTELLIGENCE SUMMARY.

Army Form C. 2118.

Place	Date	Hour	Summary of Events and Information	Remarks and references to Appendices
PIEBROUCK	11.3.17		The Brigade moves to another area, a few miles west of HAZEBROUCK. The Company also the march well, to new billets at new billets good.	
Sheet 36A 1/40,000 WELLON CAPEL C4 B.0.6	12.3.17		The morning was spent in cleaning equipment etc. The C.O. inspected the Company in full marching order at noon. The turnout was satisfactory. Articles of kit were issued during the afternoon.	
	13.3.17		In the morning Physical Training, Arms drill, embussing Ammunition Supplyets. Best filling by hand and machine, and a short route march in skeleton order. To practice a smart step and strict march discipline. Football played in the afternoon. C.O's Conference at Brigade.	
	14.3.17		Training by Company indication and recognition of Targets & Advanced Gun drill. Football match played against 10th Cheshire Regt. in afternoon. Result 3 , 2 in favour of 10th Cheshires.	
	15.3.17		A Scheme took place in the morning in conjunction with 7th Trench Mortar Battery, 7th M.G. Coy. Less one section held the line from CHATEAU en C44 to X roads in E3 central. The Trench Mortar Battery and one M.G. Section with guns on pack animals attacked as a written by Director from STEENBECQUE. LA BELLE HOTESSE and X roads West of those points Forwards STEREUS. The Bn's M.G.O. C'd the operation.	

10/72134. Wt. W.2987-17/6. 500000 4/15. Sr. J. C. & L.

WAR DIARY
or
INTELLIGENCE SUMMARY.
(Erase heading not required.)

Army Form C. 2118.

Place	Date	Hour	Summary of Events and Information	Remarks and references to Appendices
Sheet 36A 1/40000				
WALLON CAPPEL C4 b0.6	16-3-17		Baths for the whole company in the morning at LYNDE, remainder of the time section at the head of section officers, kit inspection etc carried out. Brig Commander visited the transport lines. Meeting of Officers & N.C.O's to discuss yesterday's scheme.	
	17.3.17		Company paraded at 8.30 a.m. for Brigade route march. No. 2 Section with track hones formed part of Advance Guard. Rendez-vous at ROAD JN. T.22 b 94. Time of start 10 a.m. Route:- RENESCURE — CAMPAGNE — WARDRECQUES — BELLE CROIX — RACQUINGHEM — BLARINGHEM — C16a 3.5. SERCUS. Company paraded for Church Services. Roman Catholics at 8.30 a.m. Church of England at 10.45 a.m. At 2.30 p.m. a football match took place between No. 1 and 4. Sections ending in a win for No. 4.	
	18.3.17			
	19.3.17		Company paraded at 9.30 a.m. for Brigade move to BORRE area. Starting point U.24.c.3.7. The Brigade halted on the road between 10.30 a.m. to 11.15 a.m. During this halt a hot dinner was served to the Company. The Company was settled in new billets by 2.30 p.m.	
	20.3.17		The Company paraded at 9.30 under Section officers. During the morning	

Sheet 36A 1/40000

Army Form C. 2118.

WAR DIARY
or
INTELLIGENCE SUMMARY.
(Erase heading not required.)

Instructions regarding War Diaries and Intelligence Summaries are contained in F. S. Regs., Part II. and the Staff Manual respectively. Title pages will be prepared in manuscript.

Place	Date	Hour	Summary of Events and Information	Remarks and references to Appendices
Sheet 36A. 1 in 40,000				
BORRE.	(20.3.'17)		Guns, clothing and equipment were cleaned up. Also C.O. and 2 i/c Coy? reconnoitred billets in MERRIS area with a view to taking over on the following day.	
	21.3.17.		The Brigade moved from BORRE to MERRIS area this morning. The Machine Gun Company moving independently. Company paraded outside billets at 8.20 a.m. and passed starting point (ROAD JN. E.22.9.5.5) at 9 a.m. It then proceeded to new billets in BLEU village (Fig b & Fig d) via VIEUX BERQUIN arriving at 10.10 a.m. The remainder of the day was spent in general cleaning up of billets, clothing, equipment etc.	
BLEU	22.3.17.		Company paraded at 7 a.m. for half an hour's Physical Training. During the morning guns and gun equipment were cleaned and packed, billets overhauled and all limbers cleaned and oiled. During the afternoon a football match took place between Head Quarters and No.4. Section resulting in a win for No.4.	
	23.3.17.		~~The~~ During the morning, billets were cleaned out, blankets rolled, and general preparations made for moving. The Company paraded	

Army Form C. 2118.

WAR DIARY
or
INTELLIGENCE SUMMARY.
(Erase heading not required.)

Instructions regarding War Diaries and Intelligence Summaries are contained in F.S. Regs., Part II. and the Staff Manual respectively. Title pages will be prepared in manuscript.

Place	Date	Hour	Summary of Events and Information	Remarks and references to Appendices
Sheet 28 1:40,000 FME. DU BOIS.			at 10.25 am. and marched to FME. DU BOIS. A19b via (Sheet 36A) HTE. MAISON F14d and PTE. FME. DU BOIS. F22d. Arrival in new billets 12.30 p.m. Remainder of day spent in cleaning up billets.	
Sheet 36NW 1:20,000 BLANCHE MAISON. A8d.	24.3.17		Company paraded at 9 am for cleaning guns, gun equipment and limbers and dismissed at 10.30. Remainder of morning was spent in packing up and preparation for move to a new area. Dinners served at 12.30 p.m. Company paraded ready to move off at 2 p.m., and arrived at new billets (BLANCHE MAISON. A8.) at 2.45 p.m.	
	25.3.17		Church parade with D Company Loyal North Lancashire Regiment at 10 a.m. At 2.30 p.m. a football match took place between officers and sergeants, and remainder of Company, which resulted in a win for the latter.	
	26.3.17		Early morning parade cancelled on account of bad weather. Time was spent in cleaning out billets instead. Morning parades:- 9-10 a.m. mechanism and stripping. 10.15-11.15 a.m. Gun drill. 11.30-12.30 p.m. Instruction in use of Range finder. There was an issue of kit to Nº 3	

Army Form C. 2118.

WAR DIARY
or
INTELLIGENCE SUMMARY.
(Erase heading not required.)

Instructions regarding War Diaries and Intelligence Summaries are contained in F. S. Regs., Part II. and the Staff Manual respectively. Title pages will be prepared in manuscript.

Place	Date	Hour	Summary of Events and Information	Remarks and references to Appendices
Sheet 36 NW. 1:20,000. BLANCHE MAISON. A8d.	(26.3.17)		3 & 4 Sections between 9.30 and 10.30 a.m. The Commanding Officer lectured Sergeants and Corporals on "Maps and Compass" at 10.30 a.m. and held an examination for promotion of all Lance Corporals at 11 a.m. The Company paraded at 2 p.m. and marched to Divisional Gas School at MERRIS for testing box respirators and exchanging defective ones.	
	27.3.17		Company paraded at 9 a.m. under Section Officers. Morning parades:- 9-10. Firing Stoppages. 10.15-11.15" Advanced drill and use of auxiliary mounting. 11.30-12.30 Mechanism. During the afternoon, a Rugby football match took place.	
	28.3.17		Early morning parade, 7 a.m. – 7.30 a.m. Physical Training. Company paraded at 9 a.m. for cleaning limbers, gun Equipment, etc. also preparation of stoppage belts. At 12.30 p.m. Company and fighting limbers moved off to Range at (MAP. 28 S.W. 1:20,000) S 27 b. The following practices were fired. Grouping, stoppages, practice wearing P.H. helmet, practice with auxiliary mounting. Company stood to after that all ranks were	

Army Form C. 2118.

WAR DIARY
or
INTELLIGENCE SUMMARY.
(Erase heading not required.)

Instructions regarding War Diaries and Intelligence Summaries are contained in F. S. Regs., Part II. and the Staff Manual respectively. Title pages will be prepared in manuscript.

Place	Date	Hour	Summary of Events and Information	Remarks and references to Appendices
MAISON BLANCHE.			Practical in use of neutrum. Six rounds per man were then fired. Company returned to MAISON BLANCHE at 4.30 pm. At 10.30 am. all Lance Corporals were examined in drilling. For this purpose No 4. Section turned out in clean fatigue dress with belts.	

Douglas Spark
MAJOR,
COMMDG. 7th MACHINE GUN COY.

No. 7 MACHINE GUN COMPANY.
No. X
Date. 28.3.17.

Army Form C. 2118.

WAR DIARY
or
INTELLIGENCE SUMMARY.
(Erase heading not required.)

Nr Maxim Gun Coy

Vol 16

Place	Date	Hour	Summary of Events and Information	Remarks and references to Appendices
HOUPLINES. 36 NW. 1:10000.				
LE BIZET. C 13 d.	5.4.17		No 1 Section and No 2. Section relieved the Australians in RIGHT and CENTRE Sectors respectively same evening. Also 1 gun of No 3 Section relieved the team at LANCASHIRE COTTAGE.	
	6.4.17		Morning was spent in taking over billets from 11th Aus. Company, and general cleaning. Also the bath-house was started. C.O. and 2nd i/c reconnoitred defences of Right, Centre and Left Sectors today.	
	7.4.17		Gun teams out of the line spent the forenoon on gun drill, mechanism etc. In the afternoon all men had baths, and change of clothing. In the forenoon, guns out of the line were prepared for relief in the evening of Right Sector. Also of the two guns in Left Sector. At 4.30 p.m., No 4 Section night bus one team moved off to relieve Right Sector except No 4 F.M. Gun, which was relieved by remaining team of No 4 Section after dark. The two teams of No 3 Section out of the line relieved the two teams in at 4.30 p.m.	
	8.4.17		Church Parades in LE BIZET for teams out of the line :- PRESt 11 a.m. Church of England 10 a.m. The Commanding Officer attended a conference of M.G. Company Commanders held by the Corps M.G. Officer in BAILLEUL	

WAR DIARY or INTELLIGENCE SUMMARY

Army Form C. 2118.

Place	Date	Hour	Summary of Events and Information	Remarks and references to Appendices
HOUPLINES 36 N.W 1:10,000				
LE BIZET C.13.d.	8-4-17		this afternoon. There was an issue of kit and clothing to teams out of the line this afternoon.	
	9-4-17		Section out of the line sent out during the morning also some articles of kit issued. In the afternoon C.O. & 2nd i.C visited the line. Snipers suspected to be withdrawing but patrol reports front line still held. C.O. visited 2nd and 1st Wilts during evening to ascertain the situation reported by patrol.	
	10-4-17		A quiet day – In the morning the C.O. visited the guns in the left sector. In the afternoon the relief took place, the two guns of No. 3 sect. relieving the two guns in the line, No. 1 sect relieved No. 2 sect. The rural indirect fire gun claimed at the enemy artillery appeared to be searching for RESERVE FARM GUN.	
	11-4-17		During the morning the C.O. issued articles of clothing to the men out of the line. In the afternoon the C.O. visited the gun in the centre sector. More artillery activity to-day on the front of the enemy, who shelled the neighbourhood of LANCASHIRE SUPPORT FARM and also LE TOUQUET STATION.	

WAR DIARY or INTELLIGENCE SUMMARY

Army Form C. 2118.

Place	Date	Hour	Summary of Events and Information	Remarks and references to Appendices
HOUPLINES 36 NW 1:10,000				
LE BIZET C.13.d	12-4-17		The C.O. visited the line with the Brigade Major this morning & this afternoon. Visited the transport & flying out the men. 2nd i/c visited guns in Right Sector.	
			LE TOUQUET STATION was shelled during the day in 5th and the neighbourhood of RESERVE FARM, GUN & LANCASHIRE COTTAGE. C.O. officers on rounds to RESERVE U.K.	
	13-4-17		Enemy artillery has been fairly active to-day. At 6.30 p.m. he shelled LE BIZET in the neighbourhood of the Convent & (part) some casualties. 2nd A.C. visited.	
			The gun in Left Sector this afternoon. LANCASHIRE COTTAGE gun (have) to LAWRENCE FM U47088	
			on account of continuous shelling of the previous position.	
	14-4-17		No 4 Sect. fired out during the morning. In the afternoon 2nd i/c visited the gun in the Right Sector. Enemy artillery quieter to-day. Enemy	
			aeroplane flew very low over PONT NIEPPE this morning. Our aeroplanes were not active but entered. We carried out indirect fire on C.T.'s, cross roads & pontoon bridge	
	15-4-17		Normal activity to-day. In the afternoon 2/2nd i/c visited Centre Sector. We carried out indirect fire during the night on cross roads at C.11.c.35.95	
			and also on pontoon bridges across the LYS. Work carried out: improvements to emplacements. After a heavy bombardment commencing 7.45 pm enemy entered our trenches at LONG. AVE. but were ejected, leaving some dead. Our casualties: 126 killed & wounded & 6 missing	

Army Form C. 2118.

WAR DIARY
or
INTELLIGENCE SUMMARY.
(Erase heading not required.)

Instructions regarding War Diaries and Intelligence Summaries are contained in F. S. Regs., Part II. and the Staff Manual respectively. Title pages will be prepared in manuscript.

Place	Date	Hour	Summary of Events and Information	Remarks and references to Appendices
HOUPLINES. 36NW. 1:10.000. LE BIZET. C/3.d.	16-4-17		No 4. Section + 2 teams of No 3 Section, relieved No 1 Section + 2 teams of No 3 Sect. During the afternoon. Clothing + equipment issued to No 4. Section during the morning. 2nd i/c visited the Right Sector	
	17-4-17		2nd i/c visited the Right Sector during the morning. Very quiet during the day	
	18-4-17		Gun teams out of the line spent the forenoon on mechanism and stoppages. In the afternoon the acting C.O. visited O.C. 3rd Worcestershire Regiment in the line to arrange co-operation of infantry and machine guns in case of a raid. Company was relieved by the 75th M.G. Company. Relieving Company arrived at noon and relief was complete by 4 pm with the exception of 2 L.V.S. F.S. guns which was relieved at dusk. The Company left LE BIZET about 6 pm and marched via NIEPPE and near BAILLEUL Road to A2.d and occupied Willks H. of BLANCHE	
	19-4-17			
FRANCE Sheet 36 1:40000 BLANCHE MAISON. A & d.	20-4-17	8.30 am	MAISON by 8.30 pm. During morning general clean up of guns, kit and equipment. Company was paid at 2 pm.	

Army Form C. 2118.

WAR DIARY
or
INTELLIGENCE SUMMARY.
(Erase heading not required.)

Instructions regarding War Diaries and Intelligence Summaries are contained in F.S. Regs., Part II. and the Staff Manual respectively. Title pages will be prepared in manuscript.

Place	Date	Hour	Summary of Events and Information	Remarks and references to Appendices
FRANCE Sheet 36 1:40,000 BLANCHE MAISON. A 2 d.	21/4/17		Forenoon parades:- 7.30 am. Physical Training. 9 am - 10 am Firing Stoppages. 10 am to 11 am Advanced drill. 11.30 - 12.30 pm Mechanism. At 3 pm Company was fitted out with clothing, and small kit.	
	22/4/17		Church of England Service on Company was held with the French Master Battery was held at 11 am. The Brigadier General attended this Service. Some enemy aeroplanes appeared during the early morning and were driven off by our anti-aircraft.	
	23/4/17		N°s 1 and 2 Sections along with half the Transport paraded 7.30 am for baths at OOTRESTEENE at 9 am. Remainder of Company paraded at 8.30 am for latter. About 6 enemy aeroplanes flying very high appeared well over our lines during the forenoon. Its morning was exceedingly bright but the planes were driven off by our anti-aircraft.	
	24/4/17		Parades:- 7-7.30 am Physical Training. 9 am to 12 noon Squad drill. Firing Stoppages and advanced drill. 2 Pr. Bridges, Sgt. Hobbs and Cpl. Cochar left at 8.30 am for one day Gas Course at Div¹ Gas School at S 29 central. At 2.30 pm there was a football match between Officers + NCOs. of the Coy. V	

WAR DIARY or INTELLIGENCE SUMMARY

Army Form C. 2118.

Place	Date	Hour	Summary of Events and Information	Remarks and references to Appendices
FRANCE. Sheet 36. 1:40.000 BLANCHE MAISON. A.2.d.	(24-4-17) 25-4-17		Officers & N.C.Os. of 7th T.M.B. Report A.1. in favour of former team. Parades:- 7-7:30 Physical Training under I. orderly officer. 9—12:30pm. Indication and Recognition of Targets — Range finding — Practice in combined sights. At 2:30pm a football match took place. Officers and N.C.Os. v. remainder of Coy. Result. 1.0 in favour of latter.	
	26-4-17		Working party of 1 Officer and 52 other ranks left at 7:30am with haversack rations for all day duty on Ammunition Dump construction at B.19.a.4.4. (Sheet 36 N.W.). This was paraded by Nos. 2 and 4 Sections. Morning parades for remainder of Company:- 8:45am. Nos. 1 & 3 Sections paraded in fighting order with limbers hooked. They marched to S.27 Central where an attack scheme on MONT DE LILLE was carried out. Operation orders and sketch maps attached.	
	27-4-17		The Coy. found a working party 1 officer, 52 other ranks in the ammunition dump. The remainder of the Coy. did physical drill, gun drill (firing from mounting tripod, mechanism and stripping) and machine practice. The C.O. returned from leave.	
	28-4-17		Half the Coy. on fatigues. Remainder 9-10am. lecturing Water & Cooling into action. 11:30—2 p.m. The Coy. (less this) carried out an attack scheme in the turnip ground at MONT DE LILLE. (Orders) Acted for ci. on the Chief point practised.	

L. Dixon Lee Smith
Capt. M.G.C.

Army Form C. 2118.

7 M.G. Coy

Nov 17

WAR DIARY
or
INTELLIGENCE SUMMARY.
(Erase heading not required.)

Instructions regarding War Diaries and Intelligence Summaries are contained in F. S. Regs., Part II. and the Staff Manual respectively. Title pages will be prepared in manuscript.

Place	Date	Hour	Summary of Events and Information	Remarks and references to Appendices
STEENT-JE	Sad 29-4-17		The Coy attended church parade with the Loyal North Lancs. In the afternoon the Coy were photographed. Football in the evening. Orders received for move to STRAZEELE area.	
	30-4-17		The Company leaves for the new area 8.30 a.m. and marches via OUTTERSTENE and MERRIS to the STRAZEELE area. C.S.M. Wells arrives from the base to replace C.S.M. Jesse (returned to England as instructor.)	
Sheet 36A STRAZEELE E 12 c	1-5-17		Strength of Company 10 officers, 177 O.R. Stand off strength 7. Reinforcements 7. Cleaning and packing tin box and cleaning ammunition, marching to company. In the afternoon N.C.O's drill under the Company Sergeant Major. The Brigadier inspected the transport lines this morning.	
	2-5-17		Dismissed drill by the Company in the morning. Drill for the whole Company under the C.S.M. In the afternoon (1 hour) of instruction for N.C.O.s (Company)	
	3-5-17		In the morning squad drill under C.S.M., gun drill by section and lecture for N.C.O.s C.S.M. Strength increase – 36392 Pte Dennoly to have medically unfit Brigade Drummond Gun'M.G.O visited the Coy this afternoon.	

Army Form C. 2118.

WAR DIARY
or
INTELLIGENCE SUMMARY.
(Erase heading not required.)

Instructions regarding War Diaries and Intelligence Summaries are contained in F. S. Regs., Part II. and the Staff Manual respectively. Title pages will be prepared in manuscript.

Place	Date	Hour	Summary of Events and Information	Remarks and references to Appendices
STRAZEELE	4-5-17		Company lines for men at 8.10 a.m., marching via PRADELLES – HAZEBROUCK –	
[Mar-Hazebrouck 5A] WALLON CAPELL	5-5-17		WALLON CAPELL. Lecture in Billets men WALLON CAPELL at noon. Strength relieved C.S.M. Jesse to U.K. Company moves off at 6.40 a.m. and marches via EBBLINGHEM – ARQUES – ST OMER to QUELMES 18 miles. One man fell out on march. Billets from arrangements made to move the following day.	
QUELMES	6-5-17		Company moves off at 10.30 a.m. and marches to CORMETTE where billets are taken over from a company of the 3rd Worcester. Billets quite good.	
CORMETTE	7-5-17		Commencement of training. – Physical Training 7-7.30 a.m. Squad drill rifle & cleaning and musketry during the morning. Also fitting out men with clothes and small kit. (Drums) drill in the afternoon.	
"	8-5-17		Physical training – Company drill under C.S.M. and instruction in the use of the Lewis Gun by section officers. Lecture on looking in the afternoon at Brigade H.Q. on 'C.S.M., C.Q.M.S. and Coy. Cook lettered.) Sect officer,	
	9-5-17		Range Practice 8.30 a.m. – 3 p.m. Repeating the practice and improvising & firing with light target. Lecture in afternoon by officers and N.C.O's on the use of Lewis Defence Lay. field art by the Enemy	

T.134. Wt. W708–776. 500000. 4/15. Sr J. C. & S.

WAR DIARY or INTELLIGENCE SUMMARY

Army Form C. 2118.

Place	Date	Hour	Summary of Events and Information	Remarks and references to Appendices
Regt. HQrs HAZEBROUCK 5A CORMETTE	10-5-17		Push sentry drill followed by scheme during back times. Bath for the Coy in the afternoon. Lecture to officers at WISQUES on fighting at ST OMER in the evening.	
"	11-5-17		Physical training under C.S.M. (Drechsel) drill and fitting bombers & Lewis into action. Gunnery by sections at night. Guides were selected in the rear of the sections for to march to each of the points.	
"	12-5-17		Company drill & Lewis Gun attack scheme. (Attached scheme attached). The Brigadier was present during the commencement of the scheme. Lunch at Esquelbecq & parade service in billets. Revolver practice during afternoon.	
"	13-5-17		Reconnaissance of turning area by officers in the evening.	
"	14-5-17		Company drill. Stoppages in Short Lewis Gun mechanism. Lecture in evening. Men turn 4 P.M. – 6 P.M. Brigade night march 9 P.M. – 11.45 P.M. Each must turn to march to its assembly point by companies. The Coy pts successful in reading its correct position. Night thirty (no. 2) the Lewis Gun time light for attachment. Section attacks to battalion to attack scheme in Brigade training area.	
"	15-5-17		Each platoon Lewis whistled the men for a certain time.	
"	16-5-17		Platoon for part in Brigade attack scheme. The guns of two sections fire part of attack in sections falsing part theoretic from 3.45 a.m. the reinforcing personnel turned to carrying party for the section falsing part. Bombing & conflict in evening.	

WAR DIARY
or
INTELLIGENCE SUMMARY.
(Erase heading not required.)

Army Form C. 2118.

Place	Date	Hour	Summary of Events and Information	Remarks and references to Appendices
Reg. Mah. HAZEBROUCK FA CORMETTE	17-5-17		The Company took part in Brigade attack scheme in the morning. Consolidation being the chief role of the machine guns. M.G. work carried out by Sub Section Commanders from N.C.O.'s and 5.6 men attached to the Bn from the Coy. Bearing Competition in the evening Sixty men attached to the Coy from the Batt in Company trained at 7 a.m and marched via TATINGHEM, ST.OMER, ARCQUES,	
EBBLINGHEM	18-5-17		to EBBLINGHEM, where they were billeted in the Platoon for the night. Company turned out during the afternoon.	
STRAZEELE	19-5-17		Company turned out at 8.10 a.m (am) (marched) via HAZEBROUCK to the STRAZEELE area & were billeted there for the night. The following ammunitions have taken place, extract London Gazette dated 27-4-17 Temp 2/Lt G.A. Mallinson to be Temp Lieut from	
	20-4-17		April. Oct 1917. Temp 2/Lt S.T. May to be Temp Lieut	
Reg. Mah Sheet 28 S.W.	20-5-17		Company turned 8.30 a.m & marched to Erquinghem at Sig a 7.2 arriving the about 2 p.m.	
	21-5-17		Billoraks here to work the field. Issue of Kit to the company in the evening Two Sterling (parts form)	
	22-5-17		Plan of instruction for attached men under Lieut Jennes M.C. begun. The C.O. and Section Officers reconnoitre trenches leading up to the line. Some of the attached men being unfit for the work required of them have been sent back to battle & reflum by others.	

T.134. Wt. W708-776. 500000. 4/15. Sir J. C. & S.

WAR DIARY
or
INTELLIGENCE SUMMARY.
(Erase heading not required.)

Army Form C. 2118.

Place	Date	Hour	Summary of Events and Information	Remarks and references to Appendices
	23/5/17		Class paraded during morning & afternoon for further instruction under Lieut Jenner. Selions paraded for general cleaning of guns etc in anticipation of move	
	24/5/17		Selions paraded for cleaning guns etc preparing for going into the trenches. Class of instruction took place in the morning. The whole Company rested in the afternoon & evening. At 12 midnight the Coy paraded to move up to the line. Coy marched to Coy HQrs situated at T.20.C.3.0. about 28 S.N. - a farm in NIEPPE - NEUVE EGLISE road. where Nos 1, 3 & and 4 had ten rd. Three sections then marched up & took over from the 74th M.G. Coy in the NULVERGHEM sector.	
T.20.C.3.0.	25/5/17		Class paraded under Lieut Jenner for further instruction. The attached men & Lieut Jenner did not go into the trenches but stayed at Coy HQrs & to carry on training. The CO with Mr Lovell carried out a complete reconnaissance of the sector returning to Coy HQrs about 6.30 pm.	
	26/5/17		Class paraded under Lt Jenner for further instruction.	

Place	Date	Hour	Summary of Events and Information	Remarks and references to Appendices
	26/5/17		In the afternoon the C.O made another reconnaissance of the line returning back at Coy H.Qrs about 7.30 p.m. At 9.15 p.m. the men at H.Qrs (No 2 sec., part of No 4 sec & the attached men) were fried out.	
	27/5/17		The class fired stoppages on the range. The firing showed universal progress after and a short period of instruction. In the afternoon at 2 p.m. there was a meeting of M.G. Coy. Comdrs. Div. M.G.O at our H.Qrs. At 6 p.m. C.O attended a Conference at Bde. H.Qrs. At 6.15 p.m. men attached to Nos 1 & 2 sec. proceeded up the line to be shown round. Reinforcements also went returning about 6.45 p.m. No. 2 sec relieved No. 3 sec in the line about 9 p.m. 2nd Lieut. Dickenson took over charge of Lewis Tradesmen somewhat delayed owing to a stoppage on the roads eventually reaching Coy HQrs about midnight	

WAR DIARY
or
INTELLIGENCE SUMMARY
(Erase heading not required.)

Army Form C. 2118.

Place	Date	Hour	Summary of Events and Information	Remarks and references to Appendices
	28/5/17		C.O. went up the line in the morning inspecting the Lewis Gun positions. All officers attended a lecture on Machine Gun Barrages by Corps M.G.O. Col Applin. In the evening the C.O. held an officers meeting. The attacked men paraded under Lieut Jenner in the morning — the class was then dispersed & the men belonging to Nos 1 & 2 sec went up to join their sections.	
	29/5/17		Shell exploded near front line gun killing two men wounding S/Sgt Homan. Owing to heavy guns being placed just in rear of our indirect gunpositions have started to make new positions for the guns.	

Douglas Park MAJOR,
COMDG 7th MACHINE GUN COY.

Army Form C. 2118.

WAR DIARY
or
INTELLIGENCE SUMMARY.
(Erase heading not required.)

7th Machine Gun Company

Vol 18

Place	Date	Hour	Summary of Events and Information	Remarks and references to Appendices
Sheet 28 S.W.				
Comp. H.Q. 720 C53	24-5-17		C.O. paid first visit to Division in TLC. Nos 1 and 2 Section in the Line (WULVERGHEM Sector) Working parties from No 4 Sect. sent up to the Line to build indirect fire position for Sect. guns in preparation for the day of the assault on MESSINES RIDGE. No 2 Sect. have 2 men killed and two wounded by entering wrong gun position area.	
WULVERGHEM	30-5-17		Working party carried a very successful shoot, finished the position. No 3 Sect. & eight pack horses carry up 506,000 rounds S.A.A. to the indirect fire battery position.	
	31-5-17		Indirect fire battery position completed & selected, filling shelter, & telephone dugout finished by telephone communication established.	
	1-6-17		At Zero All of No 2 Sect. billets near NORTH MIDLAND FARM 9.1 men shell sheard Nos 1 & 2 Sect. relieved by No 3 & 4 Section in early morning. No 2 Sect. had 2 men killed & two wounded at NORTH MIDLAND FARM, No 4 Sect. two men. Three men killed & two wounded in the above disaster.	
	2-6-17		Preliminary Conference of Officers in the above of 1g/s Gun Company (7.M.M.G3). No 4 Sect. relieved by 1st gun of 1g/s Gun Company. No 3 Sect. gun position with indirect fire & lanes by 3rd WORCESTERS & 8th L.N. LANCS Regt; further finishes were achieved.	

WAR DIARY or INTELLIGENCE SUMMARY.

Army Form C. 2118.

Place	Date	Hour	Summary of Events and Information	Remarks and references to Appendices
WULVERGHEM Sector	3-6-17		No 3 Sect. detached to a Sect. of 7th M.G. Coy. The whole company moved to bivouac on REVELSBERG HILL at T.17.c.4.9. The C.O. & 2IC Rideren up to the line to arrange with the Bn. to co-operate in raid by 1st Wilts (Rev)	
	4-6-17		Unsuccessful Rehearsing of tenders, etc. By bundles in the afternoon each man carrying exactly what he will carry in the attack.	
	5-6-17		Speech by the Brigadier to the assembled Servts. on the forthcoming attack. Conference of C.O's and 2nd I.C's at Brigade H.Q. The C.O. held a conference of all officers & N.C.O's. In the evening, to whom the attack in detail was explained. Steel helmets repainted & scrubbed. Field dressings & iodine etc. made up.	
	6-6-17		Company prepared to move. 2nd I.C. reconnoitering the route to position of assembly. Limbers (12 loaded) 2.30 hr. G.S. waggon & cookers, a short speech by the C.O. moved up to position. The limbers brought up the guns to SOUVENIR FARM T5.c.5.6 then eventually handover.	

Army Form C. 2118.

WAR DIARY
or
INTELLIGENCE SUMMARY.
(Erase heading not required.)

Place	Date	Hour	Summary of Events and Information	Remarks and references to Appendices
WULVERGHEN SECTOR	7/6/17		Previous to Zero day I issued instructions to Officers NCO's and men as to how casualties Ray guns would got to their position. We also carrying books we went to Stike, also digging implements for and after coming into action No 3 Section Previous to zero this section of 4-guns was in position in FUSALIER TRENCH and had placed their guns, ammunition, and gun kit out in front so that no time would be wasted in getting out. At zero a mine went up and no one knew about this it caused a considerable amount of swearing as a number of men amongst the infantry got out behind, or parts of our tunnel fell in. Lieut Fay & Sgt O'Hare who had got out came back and gathered the men and brought them on and followed up the Pk Lanor. Lieut Rang took his two guns up and placed them in position about 300 yds east of the enemy old support line, and as soon as the infantry had passed opened fire on the next slope of the ridge, and on the enemy helping as far as possible with the advance and ceased fire when the barrage accorded the crest. At Zero plus 30, Lieut Rang again moved his two guns forward to positions about 200 yds east of OCCUR SUPPORT and arranged for them to open fire and consolidate the near side of the ridge.	

WAR DIARY
or
INTELLIGENCE SUMMARY.
(Erase heading not required.)

Army Form C. 2118.

Place	Date	Hour	Summary of Events and Information	Remarks and references to Appendices
			The other two guns under Lieut. Tay got into position and opened fire on the other ridge, and then moved forward to positions commanding the ridge and near slope. Emplacements were at once dug, and L/Cpl. Wickford found a dug-out containing two of the enemy, whom he rushed and captured. 2 Guns of No.1 Section & 2 Guns of No.2 Section. Previous to zero 6 guns of this section were in position at T5.2.50, 16.15 & 52. and at zero laid down a barrage on the slope W. of OCTOBER TRENCH firing on this until zero plus 45 minutes. I examined the hill and it is simply plastered with bullets and I think it impossible for the enemy to have passed. On receipt of message that OCTOBER TRENCH was taken guns moved forward to ONSLOE TRENCH & thence moved to a line on OXONIE STRONGPOINT BELL FARM LINE and prepared S.O.S. Barrage on line from DESPAGNE FARM NORTHWARDS. Positions were consolidated and all arrangements made for defence. 2nd Lieut. Lovell went forward to the top of the ridge just behind the 1st Wilts. and established communication with the Barrage guns giving information when the line of posts was taken, and	

WAR DIARY or INTELLIGENCE SUMMARY

having choroughly up to the ridge. Lieut. Powell took one of the guns of the 95th Coy, & himself fired on about 20 of the enemy he saw running back - to Lt. ol. Coot. R.O.(?) of Pers.

NO 4 SECTION. Previous to ZERO the 4 guns and teams were in FUSALIER TRENCH right of PILLROAD. Some guns and the being laid on the parapet. As soon as the Worcesters moved the station gol. over and followed close over. The 1st & 2nd Guns and teams went with the 10/12 Cheshires & followed them to OCCUR SUPPORT, where one gun was knocked out, the remaining three went among the 1st Wilts. On gun pushed on very rapidly on the right where there were no infantry, & fired into five parties of the enemy who seemed to be gathering together, probably with the intention of counter-attacking. Many casualties were inflicted, & the rest were driven into shell holes where they surrendered. The two guns on the left got up very close to our barrage, & found the 1st Wells had to come back into OCTOBER TRENCH. owing to our own barrage, which was still on OCTOBER SUPPORT. They dug in in front of OCTOBER TRENCH defending the line & left flank.

WAR DIARY or INTELLIGENCE SUMMARY

Army Form C. 2118.

One gun fired on a party of the enemy retreating causing them a few casualties, & the remainder to take cover in shell holes where they were eventually captured. As soon as the 1st Welsh got into OCTOBER SUPPORT they took up positions on the line helping to consolidate it. Lieut. Maddison captured a German Machine Gun when the enemy Lieut Off. fired it with good effect. Offr. having turned it round. I needed OCTOBER TRENCH just as Lieut Maddison ceased fire. I ordered one gun to be moved up from No 3 Section, but finding it was not necessary Reed it sent back. The Officers displayed considerable initiative & the men great courage & endurance with their heavy loads which they carried over broken ground. Rations, water & ammunition were sent up by Lieut Williamson to a point just short of OCTOBER TRENCH. All arrangements worked perfectly & our casualties were not heavy. During the morning Coy. Hdqrs were moved up to a German dug out on road near BELLTAR M. In this dug-out we captured two prisoners. The guns are now distributed as follows :- 3 guns in front of OCTOBER SUPPORT east of FOUR HUNS FARM — 2 guns east of

WAR DIARY or INTELLIGENCE SUMMARY

Army Form C. 2118.

Place	Date	Hour	Summary of Events and Information	Remarks and references to Appendices
			HELL FARM & two north of BELLFARM, also on Barrage gun dug in at O.31.a.6.3. to put a barrage on front of OCTOBER RESERVE & then to defend the Ridge. Three guns formed the line of defence & were which to cooperate with guns on Post flanks. Ammunition water supply etc was sent up on pack horses & definite orders issued for the defence of the various lines. In front of us a number of guns belonging to the 13th Australian Coy.	
	8/6/17		Shelling continues very heavily, but owing to the guns being sited away from trenches, & to our not allowing men to move about, the emplacements, they have not be shelled. During the day we fired on a number of German parties.	
	9/6/17		The German continues firing a lot of shells over various parts. In the evening I relieved with No 3 Section, 5 guns of the 75th M.G. Coy in the line of Out-posts, north of DESPAGNE FARM. These guns had a good field of fire, but are very badly sited — have rearranged them getting much better cooperation	
	10/6/17		Gun No 1384 received a direct hit, & is blown practically to bits.	

WAR DIARY or INTELLIGENCE SUMMARY

Army Form C. 2118.

Place	Date	Hour	Summary of Events and Information	Remarks and references to Appendices
			Lewis gun remains to 1.0.M. C.O. of the 32 M.G. Coy & the C.O. of the 13th Aust. M.G. Coy called to arrange a relief. The 32nd Coy are to take over from the 7th Coy & also from the 13th Australian Coy. The relief however was cancelled, & I relieved 3 guns of the 13th Aust. Coy in positions near O28.c08. If the positions very little work has been done – there is no cover to the Australian low ten moving about. As a result two guns and tripods were blown to pieces – three men killed & 3 wounded. This occurred on the 11th. The enemy continue fairly active with heavy shells, but very few light ones, what seem to indicate that he is withdrawing his light guns.	
	12/6/17		Guns were relieved at 11 p.m. by the 32nd M.G. Coy & marched to camp near Nieuwe Eglise.	
	13/6/17		2 + 4 Sections dig overhead fire positions at U4.c.1.9. under considerable artillery fire. Lieut. Powell wounded.	
	14/6/17		2 + 4 Sections do overhead barrage fire during the advance – the barrage being put down on a line from U.6 Central to U.12 Central. Lens 7.30 p.m. till 10 p.m. The 8 guns took over battle positions in outpost from the 74 M.G. Coy.	

DATE	
	75K Bde holding the front line what runs through GAPAARD, STEIGNAST FARM & FARM DE LA CROIX.
15/6/17	Fairly continuous shelling all day 5.9" & heavier shells used. at 9 p.m 2+4 Sections relieved by 1+3 Sections.
16/6/17	The usual shelling all day – guns mounted for anti-aircraft work.
17/6/17	Hostile shelling slightly decreased in intensity – anti-aircraft mountings removed from Bde & erected in shell holes alternative position also constructed.
18/6/17	1+3 Sections relieved at 9.30 p.m by 2+4 Sections. Hostile aeroplanes engaged during the evening.
19/6/17	Hostile aeroplanes again engaged & prevented from flying low – one was forced to return behind his own lines.
20/6/17	Nothing of importance occurred. – more shrapnel used by the enemy.
21/6/17	Relieved by 9th Aust. M.G.Coy. at 9 a.m. Company marched to camp at RAVELSBERG, & erected tents and bivouacs.
BELGIUM & FRANCE. Sheet 28. S.17.c.	
22.6.17	

Place.	Date.	
BELG. & FRANCE Sheet 28. S17c. RAVELSBERG.	23.6.17	Company paraded at 9.15 am. for C. of E. Service in Camps at 9.30 am. During the afternoon a number of enemy aeroplanes came over & brought down 3 of our observation balloons. All the enemy planes got away safely. About 7 p.m. another enemy plane came over & was forced to land well behind our lines. At 9 p.m. Company paraded for march to billets in VERTE RUE ½ mile S.W. of
Sheet HAZEBROUCK Ed. 2. 1:100000.		VIEUX BERQUIN, arriving at 1 am.
VIEUX BERQUIN.	24.6.17	Company paraded from 11.30 am. to 12.30 p.m. for cleaning up of harness & gun equipment. Rolls for all deficiencies were nominated by Section officers. 2.30-3.30 p.m. continuation of harness cleaning. Company paraded at 10.15 p.m. for march via LE SART, to billets near HAVERSKERQUE. Arrived in billet by 3 am.
HAVERS-KERQUE.	25.6.17	Company paraded at 9.50 p.m. for march via BUSNES, LILLERS, ST. HILAIRE to RELY. arrived in billet at 3.30 am. It rained heavily most of the night.
RELY.	26.6.17.	Reveille at 10 am. Transport paraded at 6.30 p.m. under transport officer and general remainder of Transport in the Brigade at Fork road 600° S. of I in TIRMONDE, continuing to DELETTE on the Lys. Company paraded at 11 p.m. and marched via CUHEM & ERNY to DELETTE. Arrived in billets by 1 am.
DELETTE.	27.6.17	Reveille 12 noon. Afternoon spent in general cleaning up of billets, equipment & arms.

Place	Date.	
HAZEBROUCK 5a Ed. 2. 1:100 000. DELETTE.	28.6.17	Morning parades - 9 - 10.30 am. 11 - 12.30 pm. Morning devoted to cleaning up guns & gun equipment. At 10 am. all officers paraded mounted and rode in to COYECQUE for inspection of all officers of 7th Brigade by Major General Jacobs commanding Second Corps.

Douglas Garth
MAJOR.
COMDG. 7TH MACHINE GUN COY.

No. 7
MACHINE GUN
COMPANY.
No. W.D.
Date 29-6-17

Army Form C. 2118.

WAR DIARY
or
INTELLIGENCE SUMMARY.

(Erase heading not required.)

7th. Machine Gun Coy.

No 19

Place	Date	Hour	Summary of Events and Information	Remarks and references to Appendices
Sheet: 1:40,000 THEROUANNE R.1.Central. DELETTE.	29/6/17		Company paraded at 7.30 a.m. under Orderly Officer for Physical Training. Breakfast at 8 a.m. Forenoon parade 9 a.m. to 10 a.m. Gun Drill under Section Officers 10.15 to 11.15 a.m. Mechanism & Stoppages. 11.30 a.m. to 12.30 p.m. Belt filling by hand and machine. At 3 p.m. the Company paraded for bathing in the RIVER LYS. At 5.30 p.m. a lecture was given to the Company Subject: "Range Work." Today a Brigade class was convened for the training of P.T. Instructors. 2 officers and 4 N.C.Os were detailed to attend this class daily according to orders by Brigade.	
DELETTE.	30/6/17		Physical Training was carried out by Orderly Officer between 7 a.m. & 7.30 a.m. Forenoon parade 9-10 a.m. Issue of Clothing & equipment. 10.15-11.15 a.m. Mechanism and Stoppages. 11.30 a.m. – 12.30 p.m. Instruction in Range practice. In the evening at 5.30 a lecture was delivered to the Company. Subject:- "Machine Gun Barrage."	
DELETTE.	1/7/17		Church Parade. 9 a.m. Presbyterian and Non Conformist Services. At 11 a.m. the Commanding Officer 5 p.m. Church of England Service. inspected the Company in full marching order. At 6 p.m. a foot ball match	

WAR DIARY
or
INTELLIGENCE SUMMARY.

(Erase heading not required.)

Army Form C. 2118.

Place	Date	Hour	Summary of Events and Information	Remarks and references to Appendices
DELETTE. Sheet; THEROUANNE 1: 40,000 R.1. Central.			was played on a field outside DELETTE village. Sides, 7th Machine Gun Coy. 7th Trench Mortar Battery and Brigade H.Q. V 195th Divisional Machine Gun Company. Result 1:0 in favour of former team.	
	2/7/17		Physical Training was carried out between 7am and 7.30 am. At 9.30 a.m. Company marched to 30 x Range just outside the village, with guns + gun kit ready for firing. All men were practised in Elementary practices. Men attached from Battalions showed great keenness and aptitude. Company returned at 12.30 p.m. At 1.45 p.m. No. 1 + 2 Sections with H.Q. of transport paraded and marched to COYECQUE for baths. They were followed by 3 + 4 Sections with Headquarters at 3 p.m. At 4 p.m. N° 3 + 4 Sections were given a lecture on "Care + use of Box Respirators" by a Second Lieut N.C.O.	
	3/7/17		Training during the morning consisted of Gun Drill. - Practice in Stoppages while wearing box Respirators. - Belt filling. At 6 p.m. most of the Company attended a performance given by the 25th Divisional Pierrots at COYECQUE.	
	4/7/17		Company Route March cancelled owing to wet weather. The morning was	

Army Form C. 2118.

WAR DIARY
or
INTELLIGENCE SUMMARY.
(Erase heading not required.)

Instructions regarding War Diaries and Intelligence Summaries are contained in F. S. Regs., Part II. and the Staff Manual respectively. Title pages will be prepared in manuscript.

Place	Date	Hour	Summary of Events and Information	Remarks and references to Appendices
DELETTE Sh.17 THEROUANNE 1:40,000 R.I. Central			Spent under cover and instruction in musketry, stoppages and stripping carried	
	5.7.17		out. A football match between 7th Bde HQ (including 7 M.S. Coy) and 74th Bde HQ took place in the evening. The next day 4:1 in favour of latter team. Physical Training 9 a.m. to 10 a.m. Advanced gun drill and Range Communication apply etc. 10.15-11.15 Instruction in Table C Part II. 11.30-12.30 Idly field lectures by Machine.	
DELETTE	6.7.17		The Company paraded at 9.30 a.m. & travelled by bus to STEENBECQUE. They then marched to the village of TANNAY immediately S.W. of BOIS D'AMONT, and billeted there overnight. A number of enemy aeroplanes flew over after dark and dropped a number of bombs in the vicinity.	
Sht HAZEBROUCK 52 1:100,000 TANNAY 7.7.17			The Company fell in at 8.30 a.m. and marched to BOESINGHEM - STEENBECQUE ROAD and at a point 500* out of STEENBECQUE. They travelled thence by bus at 10.30 a.m. to a point on the main ABEELE - POPERINGHE ROAD about 1700* S.W. of POPERINGHE. From here the Company	
HALIFAX CAMP BELGIUM & FRANCE 1:40,000 Sht 28 8.7.17 H. 18. d. 9.1.			marched to HALIFAX CAMP at H.18.d.9.0. (Sheet 28. BELGIUM & FRANCE 1:40,000) C.O., 2nd in C. and Section Officers went into the trenches & visited them respectively N.9 ZILLEBEKE during the morning. Heavy firing on the Sector immediately N. of ZILLEBEKE during the morning.	

Army Form C. 2118.

WAR DIARY
or
INTELLIGENCE SUMMARY.
(Erase heading not required.)

Instructions regarding War Diaries and Intelligence Summaries are contained in F. S. Regs., Part II. and the Staff Manual respectively. Title pages will be prepared in manuscript.

Place	Date	Hour	Summary of Events and Information	Remarks and references to Appendices
BELGIUM AND FRANCE. Sheet 28 1:40,000.			The Company spent the forenoon cleaning gun site. At 4 p.m. a C.O.'s Service was held in CAMP.	
HALIFAX CAMP. H.18.d.9.1.	9/17		Morning was spent in preparing to go into the line in front of YPRES, Guns were cleaned and filled and a certain number of belt boxes set aside for the relieved Company to take over. Packs were dumped at R.N's Store by 4 p.m. and the C.O., 2nd in C. and Headquarters moved off to take over Company Headquarters from the 25th Machine Gun Company at 5:30 p.m. The Company paraded at 8:30 p.m. and moved off with their guides by Sections to GORDON HOUSE the guides from the various gun positions took the gun teams to their positions separately. Guns were carried apart as GORDON HOUSE on pack horses, all belt boxes on the line were taken over. Relief was reported complete at 11 p.m. on the 10th. 8 casualties in this Company during relief; killed 3 privates, Wounded one officer and four other ranks.	
YPRES. I.8.c.25.10.	10/17		All positions were refixed, magnetic bearings for battle and S.O.S. targets checked and stores thoroughly cleaned up. Enemy's and our artillery fairly active throughout the day & night.	

WAR DIARY or INTELLIGENCE SUMMARY

Army Form C. 2118.

Place	Date	Hour	Summary of Events and Information	Remarks and references to Appendices
YPRES. BELG. & FRANCE Sheet 28. 1:40,000 I 8 c 2.5.10.	10/7/17		During the afternoon our medium mortars fired with good effect. At 5 p.m. and again at 8.30 p.m. a squadron of enemy planes flew over our lines and were driven off by A.A. and M.G. fire. YPRES was shelled at intervals day & night.	
	11/7/17		Our own and enemy artillery active all day & night. Over 18 hostile fires on enemy front defences during the night. Enemy 77mm & 4.2" shells were fired on our front line and C.Ts. during the afternoon. About 5 p.m. our medium mortars shot 50 rounds on to enemy trenches. In the afternoon some heavy mortar fell in vicinity of MUD LANE. This trench and WEST LANE were heavily shelled at night. One enemy squadron of aeroplanes crossed our lines at 5 a.m. 11 a.m. and again at 7 p.m. and were engaged by our A.A. & M.G. fire. YPRES shelled as usual.	
	12/7/17		O.P. day, enemy trenches acted as usual. Enemy fired field guns on our front & support lines at intervals throughout the day. Our 18 pdrs. fired on his defences at night. Enemy T.M's. and our own as usual. Some enemy planes flew over our lines at 8 p.m. and were engaged by our	

Army Form C. 2118.

WAR DIARY
or
INTELLIGENCE SUMMARY.
(Erase heading not required.)

Place	Date	Hour	Summary of Events and Information	Remarks and references to Appendices
YPRES. BELGIUM AND FRANCE Sheet 28 1/40,000.	13/7/17		A.A. and Lewis guns. Naval artillery activity kept up by both sides. Our 2" mortars fired on enemy lines during the afternoon. At 7pm N° 4 Section left Company H.Q. to relieve N° 3 Section in the Right Sector.	
	14/7/17		Enemy artillery not so active as usual, but whizz bangs and 5.9" shells were directed on our C.T.s. at intervals during the day. A working party of fourteen men was sent up to Right Sector to construct M.G. positions for eight guns. At 11pm enemy shelled YPRES with gas shells and 5.9" shells. This continued at intervals till about 1 am.	
	15/7/17		Our artillery very active all day; on C.T.s. wire and battery positions. Enemy artillery also active on our trenches & back areas. Our 2" mortars fired about 100 rounds on enemy wire & front line. Enemy T.M.s. quiet. Our aircraft very active all day. A few enemy machines crossed our lines about 2.30 pm. During the night four of our guns fired on enemy roads and C.T.s.	
	16/7/17		Artillery activity as usual. Nothing unusual took place during the day. In the evening N° 3 Section relieved N° 2 Section in Left Support sector.	

WAR DIARY or INTELLIGENCE SUMMARY

Army Form C. 2118.

Place	Date	Hour	Summary of Events and Information	Remarks and references to Appendices
YPRES	17/7		The relieved Section No. 2 was very late in arriving, took at YPRES owing to shelling with gas and 5.9's. Last party of this section arrived by 4 a.m. During the day, the reserve guns were cleaned and all traces of filled. The night barrage gun positions commenced on the 14th were completed during the night.	
BELGIUM & FRANCE 28. 1/40000	18/7		Conditions normal. Owing mist and drizzle no flares were up all day. Artillery activity as usual. At 10.30 p.m. the 7th Brigade made two raids on the Brigade front. Punishing as far as the enemy support line. Eight machine guns cooperated by barraging S.O.S. and enemy map lines. Enemy shelling and ours continued as usual. Morning was cloudy but during the afternoon our batteries were able to shoot with aeroplane observation. In the evening No. 2 Section relieved No. 1 Section in the left front section.	
	19/7			
	20/7		Shelling as usual. Visibility moderate and a large number of our aeroplanes were active especially in the afternoon and evening. During 16 day No. 1 Section at Company H.Q. spent some time in strengthening cellars and fixing gas proof curtains. At night, a working party carried water and	

WAR DIARY
or
INTELLIGENCE SUMMARY.
(Erase heading not required.)

Army Form C. 2118.

Place	Date	Hour	Summary of Events and Information	Remarks and references to Appendices
YPRES. BELGIUM & FRANCE. 28 1/40,000	20/7/17		Town Support. S.A.A. to the newly constructed barrage gun positions. Guns in the line fired about 2000 rounds each one night on the following targets:- JABBER DRIVE, MENIN ROAD, JABBER AVENUE also tramlines and C.T.s.	
	21/7/17		Continuation of repairs to H.Q. cellar were carried out. Visibility good, and many of our aeroplanes active morning and afternoon. At night a working party was supplied to carry more S.A.A. to barrage positions completing each position's quota to 12000 rounds. Also transport brought up 120,000 rounds to CORDON HOUSE for use by the night firing guns. Night firing was carried out on the following targets: MENIN ROAD, & Enemy C.T.s.	
	22/7/17		Nothing to report during day. In the evening REGENT ST. in night Sector was moved to a position in BOND ST. to cover the valley on its left & so enforce the defence system. Usual night firing was carried on.	
	23/7/17		During the morning, the C.O.s of the 23rd and 24th Machine Gun Companies visited Company H.Q. to make arrangements regarding	

Army Form C. 2118.

WAR DIARY
or
INTELLIGENCE SUMMARY.
(Erase heading not required.)

Instructions regarding War Diaries and Intelligence Summaries are contained in F. S. Regs., Part II. and the Staff Manual respectively. Title pages will be prepared in manuscript.

Place	Date	Hour	Summary of Events and Information	Remarks and references to Appendices
HALIFAX CAMP. FRANCE	24/7/17		The relief of the Left and Right Sections respectively at dusk and was reported complete at 6am following morning. Sections arrived from the line at intervals during the morning, were given breakfast and retired to their huts for sleep. During the afternoon the whole Company had hot baths and change of under clothing. Pay out at 4 p.m. At 10 p.m. Cookery paraded for march to RENINGHELST area where they were accommodated in huts & tents	
Hn 8 d 9 4. Sht 28 1/40,000				
RENINGHELST C.22.C.8.7.	25/7/17		Reveille – 7.30 am. Breakfast – 8 am. Parade for cleaning of guns & equipment at 9 am. In the afternoon at 2 p.m. clothing and gun equipment were issued to replace deficiencies. At 3.15 pm the Company paraded in a field near by for Brigade inspection by G.O.C. 25th Division. At 6 p.m. the C.O. held a conference of Section officers and Section Sgts. to explain arrangements made for a coming attack.	
RENINGHELST	26/7/17		Company paraded at 10 am. for men to draw lot any to alterations in colors, the Company had to remain in Camp all	

WAR DIARY
or
INTELLIGENCE SUMMARY.
(Erase heading not required.)

Army Form C. 2118.

Place	Date	Hour	Summary of Events and Information	Remarks and references to Appendices
	27/7		morning. Company eventually moved off to field at G.27.b.7.0.40. at 2 p.m. Remainder of Company Limbs & stables were erected at 7 p.m. which company was issued with canteens to replace those already on issue for Restoration. Company paraded 10 a.m. for distribution of Divisional Congratulation Cards. Baths were available in the evening from 4 to 6 p.m.	
	28/7		The morning was given to cleaning guns etc. an Nos 3 & 4 Sections moved into the line at 4 p.m. C of C service was held prior to the Sections moving up to the line.	

R.W.Williamson Lt
t. O.C. 121 Machine Gun Coy
t 121 Machine Gun Coy

Army Form C. 2118.

WAR DIARY
or
INTELLIGENCE SUMMARY.
(Erase heading not required.)

7 try M.G.C. Vol 20

Place	Date	Hour	Summary of Events and Information	Remarks and references to Appendices
	29/7		Sections at the disposal of Section Officers during the morning. 11 a.m. Church Parade for Nonconformists & R.C.s. "B" Coy Car for ZUDEZEELE 15 at 1.45 p.m. No 3 & 4 Sections proceeded to the line in Motor Buses under Lt. J.M. Rang. at 4 p.m.	
	30/7		Transport parade 11 a.m. and move to BELGIUM CHATEAU area. Remainder of Company remaining until 11.30 p.m. then proceed to join transport. No 3 & 4 Sections in the line fire barrage for attack. Nos 1 & 2 Lieutenmann	
	31/7		New finding order for moving up to the trenches. 2/Lt. Lewis missing. No. 1 & 2 Section move up to HALF WAY HOUSE at 4 a.m. and remain there until about 5 p.m. when they proceed to relieve the 24 th M.G. Coy in the line. The rain (& shells) came down in torrents. But Cpl Section got into trenches with only one casualty. 2/Lt. Lewis reported died of wounds.	
	2/8/17		Company in the line - nothing unusual occurred, although Coy Hdq was heavily shelled.	
	3/8/17		Lt. Fanshaw (acting C.O.) goes round gun positions during the morning. Coy Hdq again shelled - dugout Lt. Ly Lell + 3 men wounded. About	

A6945 Wt. W11422/M1160 350,000 12/16 D.D.&L. Forms/C./2118/14.

WAR DIARY
or
INTELLIGENCE SUMMARY.

(Erase heading not required.)

Army Form C. 2118.

7th Coy Machine Gun Corps

Place	Date	Hour	Summary of Events and Information	Remarks and references to Appendices
		11-30 p.m.	Hdq dug-out hit by shell killing Lt Fanshawe. Lt Murdison took command until information of A.R. Fanshawe's death could be reported to R. Lang.	
	4/9		Revd. Lang takes command of the Company, and Coy Hdq moves to HALFWAY HOUSE	
	5/9		Lt. Lang, now C.O. goes round the gun positions, and No 3th Section relieve No. 1 & 2 sections in the line, also proceed to PIONEER CAMP	
	6/9		Coy Hdq move from line to PIONEER CAMP arriving there about 8 a.m. Capt Coey reports from M.G.Coy & takes over command of this Coy. Lt Lang resumes duties of temporary second in command.	
	7/9		Nos 1 & 2 Sections now out of the line, at the disposal of Section Officers during the morning. Coy Company have baths at 6 p.m. Capt. Coey visits gun positions	
	8/9		No 3th Sections in the line are relieved by No. 1 & 2 Sections respectively at 5-30 p.m.	
	9/9		Sections at the disposal of Section Officers during the morning. Best respirators are inspected. No. 3th Section bath during the afternoon.	

WAR DIARY or INTELLIGENCE SUMMARY

Army Form C. 2118.

4th Coy Machine Gun Corps

Place	Date	Hour	Summary of Events and Information	Remarks and references to Appendices
	10/8/17		Nos 1 + 2 Sections in the line fire barrage for attack (which was successful) and were relieved by No 3 + 4 Sections about 7 p.m.	
	11/8/17		Nos. 1 + 2 Section move to STEENVOORDE leaving present position at 11 p.m. No 1 + 2 Section arrived at STEENVOORDE about 2 a.m. Laing Barralled by Motor Lorries. No: 3 + 4 Sections still in the line nothing unusual occurred. C.O. visits gun in line during the afternoon.	
	12/8/17		The two Sections at STEENVOORDE at the disposal of Section Officers during the day. German aeroplane after a combat with one of ours was defeated and brought down in each lines. C.O. visits sections in trenches at 5 a.m.	
	13/8/17		No: 3 + 4 Section in the line expecting relief at 7 a.m. which does not arrive until 7 p.m. when they proceed to PIONEER CAMP, and spent there that night. Two guns under 2nd Lt Dobson detailed for anti-aircraft work (H.13. Central)	
	14/8/17		Transport paraded at 8 a.m. & move to STEENVOORDE. The remainder of the Company following at 11 a.m. No: 1 + 2 Section at the disposal of Section Officers.	
	15/8/17		Usual P.T. and R.O's inspection. All men with foot clothing fitted out with new.	

WAR DIARY
or
INTELLIGENCE SUMMARY.

4th Coy Machine Gun Corps

Army Form C. 2118.

(Erase heading not required.)

Place	Date	Hour	Summary of Events and Information	Remarks and references to Appendices
	16/7		Usual P.T. and C.O's inspection also Box respirator drill. Lieut L H Lang was appointed 2nd in-command of the Company.	
	17/7		Physical training in the morning at 11. a.m. Half the Company had Baths at 2 P.M. The other Half Company have baths.	
	18/7		The usual Training Parades	
	19/7		The Company paraded at 6.40 a.m. + marched to new area arrive at new camp about 12 noon. but found the Company we were relieving still in the huts the Company remain in the field until 4 P.M. + move into the huts then.	
	20/7		In the morning P.T. 9.30 a.m to 12.30 P.m. the Sections at-	

Army Form C. 2118.

WAR DIARY
or
INTELLIGENCE SUMMARY.

9th Coy Machine Gun Corps

(Erase heading not required.)

Instructions regarding War Diaries and Intelligence Summaries are contained in F. S. Regs., Part II. and the Staff Manual respectively. Title pages will be prepared in manuscript.

Place	Date	Hour	Summary of Events and Information	Remarks and references to Appendices
	20/8/17		The disposal of Section Officers at 2 P.m. C.O's inspection	
	21/8/17		The two teams of MoS Section relieved from Anti-Air Craft work by two teams of the same Section, at about 10 P.m. a Hun Airoplane came over and bombed our camp. Lieut Bridger wounded, and 10 men, none serious.	
	22/8/17		Physical training during the morning, at 9.30 a.m. The C.O. inspects Company in full Marching Order, at 2 P.m. Tapks on Squad Drill under C.S.M. at 8.30 P.m. Company parades, and moves to another field, in case of Camp being bombed again	
	23/8/17		The Company parades at 8 a.m. and marches to STEENVOORDE arrive at 12.30 P.m., have dinner in a field and then about 4.30 P.m. move into billits	

A6945 Wt. W11422/M1160 350,000 12/16 D. D. & L. Forms/C./2118/14.

WAR DIARY
or
INTELLIGENCE SUMMARY.

(Erase heading not required.)

Army Form C. 2118.

9th Coy Machine Gun Corps

Place	Date	Hour	Summary of Events and Information	Remarks and references to Appendices
	24/6/17		Physical training during the morning the remainder of the day, the Company on a general clean up	
	25/6/17		The usual P.T. in the morning 9-30 a.m. C.O's inspection, the rest of the forenoon, Sections at the disposal of Section Officers. 2 P.m. until 6 P.m. Company firing on range	
	26/6/17		At 6-45 a.m. 1 & 2 Sections have baths, 4-45 3 & 4 Sections and Transport have baths, Voluntary Church Service in the forenoon for R.C.'s	
	27/6/17		8-15 A.m. - 9 P.T. 9-30 - 12-30 Gun drill mechanism etc. 2 P.m - 3 Squad drill.	
	28/6/17		8-15 - 9 A.m. P.T. 9-30 - 12.30 2 - 3 Parades & Inspections.	

Army Form C. 2118.

WAR DIARY
or
INTELLIGENCE SUMMARY.

4th Bty Machine Gun Corps

(Erase heading not required.)

Place	Date	Hour	Summary of Events and Information	Remarks and references to Appendices
	29/8/17	7 a.m.	Moved coln from south of ABEELE - STEENWORDE RD. to Field 1/2 mile North of junction of above rd with Fron. Jun. C.O. 2 officers & 2 N.C.Os. reconnoitred Trench system round CLAPHAM JUNCT.	
	30/8/17	2.30 p.m.	Coy moved up to line by bus and took over from 20 m.g. Coy 8 guns in front line system. H.Q. & 6 guns in Tunnel under YPRES - MENIN RD. 2 guns in A.A. aircraft relieved by 24 m.g. Coy. Journey Transport in BELGIAN CHATEAU AREA. Relief complete 9.30 p.m. Casualties 1 officer 2/Lieut. Ward. Heavy enemy barrage during relief from Tuenal.	
	31/8/17		Night quiet - enemy effective. enemy to our rt many lights -	

E. Cott Capt.
Comdg 4 m.g. Coy

WAR DIARY or INTELLIGENCE SUMMARY

Army Form C. 2118.

767 M.G.C. Vol 21

Place	Date	Hour	Summary of Events and Information	Remarks and references to Appendices
	2/9/17		Moved camp from South of ABEELE - STEENVOORDE Rd to field ½ mile fork N. Junction of above road. C.O. 2 Officers and 21 O.R. incapacitated. Trench System round CLAPHAM JUNCTION.	
	3/9/17		Company moved up to line by Bus, and took over from 70th Machine Gun Company, 8 guns in front line system. 6 dg and 6 guns in Tunnel under YPRES - MENIN Rd. 2 guns in Anti-aircraft defence by 74th M.G.Coy. Joined Transport in BELGIUM CHATEAU AREA. Relief compt'd 9.30 p.m. Cornwallis I.O. 2nd Lieut West killed. Keary enemy barrage during relief round tunnel.	
	3/9/17		Night quiet, enemy appeared uneasy and sent up many lights.	
	4/9/17		Enemy artillery normal in the line. Bombs on right & left of tunnel occasionally allotted. About 8 p.m. the transport field was shelled, & it was found necessary to change our horse lines to an adjoining field. Slight shelling on the line, with the exception of tanks on our right & left, which	
	2/9/17		were always subject to heavy shelling. YPRES - MENIN Rd occasionally shelled.	

WAR DIARY
or
INTELLIGENCE SUMMARY.

Army Form C. 2118.

Place	Date	Hour	Summary of Events and Information	Remarks and references to Appendices
	4/9/17		Enemy Artillery active during the day. Shot 8 p.m. enemy put barrage on YPRES~MENIN Rd. Rly service 3 days in Camel overnight.	
	5/9/17		Company relieved in the line early in the morning. Party Lewis guns still however out the relief. — proceed to camp (between Vlamertinghe) Vamford Ken. O/C Lanford wounded during the march.	
	6/9/17		General cleaning up during the morning — enemy airplane very active — 8 air raid about 3 p.m.	
	7/9/17		Company moved to ABELLE area.	
	8/9/17		Cleaning up etc. 3 hours spare.	
	9/9/17		Gun drill and cleaning of Rifles during the morning — Company at rest during the afternoon. C.O. proceeds on leave to U.K.	
	10/9/17		Company proceed to EECKE area. Foot inspection on arrival in billets.	
	11/9/17		Moved to HOURELON area.	
	12/9/17		Company moved to MORIONVILLE. Foot inspection on arrival in billets.	
	13/9/17		9 to 12 noon paraded by sections for general cleaning up of equipment	

WAR DIARY
or
INTELLIGENCE SUMMARY.
(Erase heading not required.)

Army Form C. 2118.

Instructions regarding War Diaries and Intelligence Summaries are contained in F. S. Regs., Part II. and the Staff Manual respectively. Title pages will be prepared in manuscript.

Place	Date	Hour	Summary of Events and Information	Remarks and references to Appendices
	14/9/17	2 to 3 pm	Issue of Kit & Clothing. Usual training during the morning including Gun Drill, P.T. Rifle exercises etc. Games during the afternoon.	
	15/9/17		General Machine Gun Parade including instruction in Range work. Preparatory to going to the Range. 2nd Lt Pepper & 2nd Lt Potter join Company from Base Depot.	
	16/9/17		Church Parade.	
	17/9/17	7.30 to 8 am	Squad & Saluting drill. 9 am to 12.30 pm 30 yd. Range.	
	18/9/17		During the early morning the Company took train at RAIMBERT. 10 to 11 am Bell firing & instruction in range work Part II. All officers (except T.O.) and Sergeants attend Gtt Lecture at BURBURE School room at 2.15 pm on "Street fighting".	
	19/9/17		No: 1 & 2 Sections at AUCHY-au-BOIS for tactical scheme in conjunction with the 1st Welsh. No: 3 & 4 Sections usual training. 2.30 pm Company inspection — Dress fighting order.	

A6945 Wt. W14422/M1160 350,000 12/16 D. D. & L. Forms/C/2118/14

Army Form C. 2118.

WAR DIARY
or
INTELLIGENCE SUMMARY.
(Erase heading not required.)

Instructions regarding War Diaries and Intelligence Summaries are contained in F. S. Regs., Part II. and the Staff Manual respectively. Title pages will be prepared in manuscript.

Place	Date	Hour	Summary of Events and Information	Remarks and references to Appendices
	20/9/17.		Company on 200 yds range — Sections not actually firing carry out Advanced arm drill — number practice.	
	21/9/17		We play the R.A.M.C. (77 F.A.) at cricket during the afternoon, after walk in morning. Km. Competition for the Divisional Sports no training in the evening.	
	22/9/17		General parades including fighting order inspection throughout the morning. No. 3+4 Sections at AUCHY-au-BOIS No. 1 + 2 Sections usual training. Several of the Company attend the sports of the 77th F.A. during the afternoon.	
	23/9/17		Church parade. C.O. returns from leave.	
	24/9/17		7-30 to 8 am Running parade. 9 to 12-30pm Drill, Belt filling, Advancing over rough ground and use of auxiliary mounting. Lecture by Section officers on M.G. fire	
	25/9/17.		No. 1 + 2 Sections at AUCHY-au-BOIS with 3rd Worcesters. No. 1 + 2 Sections usual parades including P.T. etc.	
	26/9/17.		9/6 10 am General cleaning up. 11 am Dinners, after which men	

A6945 Wt.W1442/M1160 350,000 12/16 D. D. & L. Forms/C./2118/14.

WAR DIARY
or
INTELLIGENCE SUMMARY.
(Erase heading not required.)

Army Form C. 2118.

Place	Date	Hour	Summary of Events and Information	Remarks and references to Appendices
	29/9/17		Proceed to Divisional Lek. Ten was served on the sports ground. Usual parades, including Drill P.T. Advanced Gun Drill, Stoppages. Football match with 9th T.M.B. during the afternoon which resulted in a victory for us.	
	30/9/17		No. 2 34th Sections at PUCHY-au-BOIS. Church parades for remainder of Company.	

E. Coy Capt
Comdg 7 Coy M.S.C

WAR DIARY or INTELLIGENCE SUMMARY

Army Form C. 2118.

7 M.G. Coy. Vol 7122

7th Machine Gun Coy

Place	Date	Hour	Summary of Events and Information	Remarks and references to Appendices
	29/9/17	7 a.m.	Sections parade for baths at RAIMBERT, arriving about 10.30 a.m.	
		11 a.m.	Kit inspection by Sections. 11.30 a.m. to 12.30 p.m. Cleaning guns and repacking of fighting limbers. During the afternoon a football match was played against the 10th Cheshire Regt. - Result Chesh. 2. M.G.C.O. nil. F.W. faced member of F.G.C.M.	
	30/9/17		Usual Church parade during the morning - Holiday remainder of the day.	
	1/10/17		Company parade 8 a.m. for Quarry Range - two fighting limbers accompany the Company for carrying guns etc. - Games during the afternoon.	
	2/10/17		No: 1 & 2 Sections proceed to AUCHY-au-BOIS for tactical scheme in conjunction with the 10th Cheshire Regt. No: 3 & 4 Sections parry out the usual parades, including Gun Drill, P.T. Mechanism etc.	
	3/10/17		Early morning parade. 9 a.m. the C.O. inspects the Company in fighting order, rest of the morning - Company drill, and short Tactical scheme near Alletz. Football during the afternoon.	
	4/10/17		Company parade 9 a.m. and march to BETHUNE, arriving there about noon. Rest of the day Company at rest.	

Army Form C. 2118.

WAR DIARY
or
INTELLIGENCE SUMMARY.
(Erase heading not required.)

Instructions regarding War Diaries and Intelligence Summaries are contained in F. S. Regs., Part II. and the Staff Manual respectively. Title pages will be prepared in manuscript.

Place	Date	Hour	Summary of Events and Information	Remarks and references to Appendices
	5/10/17	8 a.m.	C.O., Section Officers and one N.C.O. per section proceed to reconnoitre the trenches (GIVENCHY SECTOR). The Company meanwhile prepare for moving into the trenches. 1-30 p.m. Parade and march to trenches and relieve the 6th R.E. Coy in the line. (Coy H.Qrs at LEPLANTIN, and Transport GORRE.) Enemy very quiet during the relay.	
	6/10/17		Enemy artillery quiet throughout the day. Hostile machine guns occasionally quiet. — Hostile m/G fire fairly active, but affair events. Our M.G. fired occasionally during the night. Work: Clearing out emplacements.	
	7/10/17		Enemy artillery and T.M. very quiet. Our artillery active throughout the day. Our M.G. quiet. Hostile aeroplane over our line in the early morning.	
	8/10/17		Enemy artillery quiet. T.M. fairly active on our front line. Enemy Machine Guns fired occasionally during the night. Our M.G. active. Enemy aircraft air relief Ranworth.	
	9/10/17		Enemy artillery and T.M. normal. Our artillery quiet. T.M. quiet. Machine guns fired during the night. Work repairing emplacements.	

WAR DIARY
or
INTELLIGENCE SUMMARY.
(Erase heading not required.)

Army Form C. 2118.

Place	Date	Hour	Summary of Events and Information	Remarks and references to Appendices
	10/5/17		Our Artillery was much more active than usual, especially early this morning - Shelled sector in front of Canadian Orchard. - Our M.G's fired during the night. Targets engaged:- Gunadier Guns at A.3.b.20.28. fired 1000 rounds on turntable at M11.a.56.03. Jew Col. Gun fired 750 rounds at A.+ B. 7.00. (Sunol Railway) Vickers Gun engaged Target at M11.a.57.53. (Turntable). Work improving night firing positions.	
	11/5/17		Artillery quiet on both sides. Enemy M.G's very quiet - an occasional shot fired. Our M.G's fired harassing fire during the night on the following TARGET. ROUNDS FIRED. Targets:- QUINQUE RUE GUN - Brickfield at A.M.8. 750. STEWART FARM " Turntable at M.2.B.72.10. 1000. NEWCOT " Forked Road at A.10.d.95.77. 1000. MOAT FARM " Wrong Farm at A.5.d. 3.75. 1000. Enemy aeroplanes fairly active all day - were fired at by our Anti-aircraft guns.	
	12/5/17		Our Artillery fired occasionally during the day. Enemy artillery very quiet. Our M.G's very quiet. Enemy M.G's fairly active enfilading QUINQUE RUE continuously. Rough at the night. Work improving night firing positions.	

WAR DIARY
or
INTELLIGENCE SUMMARY.
(Erase heading not required.)

Army Form C. 2118.

Place	Date	Hour	Summary of Events and Information	Remarks and references to Appendices
	13/10/17		Our Artillery and T.M. very quiet all day. Enemy put over some shrapnel (HE) but none fell near our position. Our M.G's engaged the following targets:-	
			TARGET — ROUNDS FIRED	
			Barton North — CONTALENT (R.11.c) — 500	
			QUINQUE GUN — PUMPING STATION — 500	
			— CROSSROAD & TRENCH TRAMWAY — 2000	
	14/10/17		Work, improving Battle emplacements. Enemy artillery fairly active during the night, in P.2.a and A.26, also on GIVENCHY & KIES P. Enemy T.M. quiet. Enemy aircraft active between 6 and 7.30 a.m. Our artillery active during day & night. Our M.G's fired in the following targets:-	
			GUN — TARGET — ROUNDS FIRED	
			MORT FARM — STRONG FARM A.5.a 30.75 — 1000	
			NEW CUT — TURN TABLE A.11.a. 59.53 — 1000	
			GRENADIER — do — 1000	
			BARNTON — CANTELEUX P.11.c. — 1000	
			QUINQUE RUE — PUMPING STATION S.29.a — 500	
			EXTREMITY — Back Road S.29.a.2.8 — 150.0	
			do — TRACKS S.23.c.15.80 — 500	
			SHETLAND — TRAMWAY A.10.a.7.8 — 2000	
			Work New emplacement for Kelly Wells. Improving trench in vicinity of	

WAR DIARY or INTELLIGENCE SUMMARY

Army Form C. 2118.

(Erase heading not required.)

Instructions regarding War Diaries and Intelligence Summaries are contained in F. S. Regs., Part II. and the Staff Manual respectively. Title pages will be prepared in manuscript.

Place	Date	Hour	Summary of Events and Information	Remarks and references to Appendices
	15/10/17		emplacements. Repairs to O.B.L. Enemy artillery fairly active, usual targets fired on during the day. O.B.L. fired on by about 12 shrapnel shells during night. Enemy T.M., about 30 medium fired in vicinity of front line, right sector about 4pm. Enemy aeroplanes over our line several times during the morning, and engaged by our A.A. M.G. fire. Our artillery active ranged on the following targets.	
			TARGET. ROUNDS FIRED.	
			GUN Enemy works at N. 29.a.2.8. 2000	
			SHIETLAND GUN " at A.4.C.51.15. 2000	
			EXTREMITY " Tramway Station. S. 29.c. 1000	
			BARTON N " Pumbling Farm. M.5.a. 30.70 1000	
			GRENADIER " Alkong Farm. M.5.a. 2000	
			MOAT FARM " Road & Tramway. A.5.a. 1250	
			NEW CUT " Track & Tramway. A.4.B. & A.5.a. 1000	
			Our aircraft active during early morning. Work completion of New emplot at KILBY WALK. Repair to approach to KINGS ROAD. Draining and cleaning trenches leading to STEWART GUN. Repairs to O.B.L.	
	16/10/17		Enemy artillery inactive. Enemy machine guns – occasional traversing fire on O.B.L. during night. Our artillery quiet. T.M. active during night.	

A6945 Wt. W14432/M1160 350,000 12/16 D.D.&L. Forms/C/2118/14.

WAR DIARY
or
INTELLIGENCE SUMMARY.
(Erase heading not required.)

Army Form C. 2118.

Place	Date	Hour	Summary of Events and Information	Remarks and references to Appendices
			Our M.G's fired a thousand rounds on each of the following targets.	
STRONG FARM (A.5.d.)			Cross Roads and Railway Junction (A.5.d.70.90). A.4.8.55.15.	
S.29.a.2.R.			A.11.a.56.5.3. CANTELEUX. Our aeroplanes were active all	
			day. Work. Improvements and repairs to dug-outs and emplacements.	
	17/10/17		Enemy artillery and T.M's quiet all day. Our M.G's engaged the usual	
			targets during the night. Work Trench + emplacements repaired, +	
			construction of new dug-out in GRENADIER RD.	
	18/10/17		Enemy artillery most active than usual. Enemy M.G's very quiet. Enemy	
			aeroplanes flew over our lines between 6 a.m + 7 a.m. Our T.M. very active	
			during the day. Our M.G's active all night + engaged the following targets.	
			CANTELEUX, PUMPING STATION S.29.B, ROAD + TRAMWAY A.4.c.55.15.	
			TOULOTTE FARM S.22.B. BRICKFIELDS. A.5.a.o.6.	
	19/10/17		Our aircraft active all day, and none night flying.	
			Enemy artillery quiet. Enemy M.G's fired occasional bursts on the QUINQUE	
			RUE. Our T.M's active during the day. Our M.G's engaged the following	
			targets. STRONG FARM. Batt Hdqr S.29.A. CANTELEUX, ENEMY TRACKS	

A6945 Wt. W14422/M1160 350,000 12/16 D.D.&L. Forms/C./2118/14

WAR DIARY
or
INTELLIGENCE SUMMARY.
(Erase heading not required.)

Army Form C. 2118.

Place	Date	Hour	Summary of Events and Information	Remarks and references to Appendices
	20/10/17		Enemy artillery active against GIVENCHY during the morning. Enemy T.M.'s active on front line between 4 & 5 p.m. Enemy M.G's fixed on fixed lines during the night on LE PLANTIN - very active on QUINQUE RUE between 5 & 8 p.m. Enemy aircraft were very active all day. Their M.G. engaged by M.G. fire with good effect. Our Artillery & T.M.'s active, fired in retaliation to enemy T.M.'s. Our M.G.'s engaged the following targets:- CANTELEUX, BRICKFIELDS, A.H.E. & P.5.A. Batt HDQ S.27.a.	
	21/10/17		Relieved by 9.5 M.G. Coy. during afternoon, and march to camp at BIEUVRY.	
	22/10/17		Cleaning equipment and clothing before breakfast. 9 to 10am Cleaning guns. 10.30 a.m. Coy inspection by C.O. 12 noon Kit inspection. Personal training during the afternoon. 7 to 8 pm Squad drill. 9 to 10 am Gun Drill (Lecture for N.C.O.'s on Barrage drill. 11am to 12.30 pm Barrage drill. Games during the afternoon.	
	23/10/17		7 to 8 pm Squad drill. 9 to 10 am Mclaren m stoppages 10 to 11 a.m. Barrage drill. 11 to 12 noon stoppages 12 to 12.30 Belt filling.	
	24/10/17			

WAR DIARY
or
INTELLIGENCE SUMMARY.
(Erase heading not required.)

Army Form C. 2118.

Place	Date	Hour	Summary of Events and Information	Remarks and references to Appendices
	25/10/17		At 1 pm 3 lorries for section (3 in all) Paraded & move into the line. Men out of the line carry out usual parades under Section N.C.O. —	
			Squad drill — P.T — Cleaning equipment & Limbers. Two men per Section having Guns detailed to learn Signalling & would along with the signallers for instruction.	
	26/10/17		Men out of the trenches do usual morning parades. — inspection in fighting order. Men in the line return to DEUVRY about 7 pm.	
	27/10/17		9 to 11 am Cleaning guns & gun equipment etc. 11 to 11.45 am Repairing Limbers. 11.45 to 12.30 pm. Belt filling. 2 to 4 pm Cleaning equipment. Lecture for All Officers at 2.30 pm on Barrage drill.	
	28/10/17		Gas Helmets inspected by Section Officers	

[signature] Capt.

Commdg 7th Machine Gun Coy

Army Form C. 2118.

WAR DIARY
or
INTELLIGENCE SUMMARY.
(Erase heading not required.)

7th Bn S. Staff. Vol 23

Instructions regarding War Diaries and Intelligence Summaries are contained in F. S. Regs., Part II. and the Staff Manual respectively. Title pages will be prepared in manuscript.

Place	Date	Hour	Summary of Events and Information	Remarks and references to Appendices
	29/12/17		Training. Weather - wind and rain.	
	30/12/17		Route march - 10 miles. 16.0 p.m. South Stafford Regt. reported for attachment. Weather - fair.	
	31/12/17		Training. All 2nd Worcesters attached, returned to Regiment. Raining. Men replaced by South Staffords. Weather - wind and rain. Preparation for trenches.	
	1/1/17		To HINNEQUIN at 2.30 p.m. Relief of 7th M.G. Coy. commenced 3.30 p.m. Hdq & 3 sections moved off. The relieving sections moved off at 5 p.m. to relieve 8 guns in forward positions. Relief of these commenced 8.45 p.m. All relief complete by 11.30 p.m. Weather, overcast - rain over night.	APPENDIX I
	2/1/17		Usual Intelligence report received 8 am. Situation normal, except for wire cutting carried out by Artillery during the afternoon. During night harassing fire carried out - 7000 rounds fired. Working party of 60 O.R. carried on work on the M.G. battery. Elsewhere usual repairs etc. carried out. Weather - murky, overcast.	

A6945 Wt. W14422/M1160 350,000 12/16 D. D. & L. Forms/C/2118/14

WAR DIARY
or
INTELLIGENCE SUMMARY.
(Erase heading not required.)

Army Form C. 2118.

Place	Date	Hour	Summary of Events and Information	Remarks and references to Appendices
	3/11/17		Situation normal, except for our artillery which carried out wire cutting during the afternoon. Working party as yesterday. Weather. Misty. overcast.	
	4/11/17		Usual Intelligence Summary received 8 am. Situation normal – enemy machine guns active during the early part of the night. Working party as yesterday. Weather. overcast.	
	5/11/17		Situation normal except for slight activity of enemy Trench Mortar. Usual night. Harassing fire carried out by our Machine Guns.	
	6/11/17		Working party as yesterday. Weather. misty. rain overnight. Situation quiet. One enemy machine gun employed on HARLEY ST active during the night. 4500 rounds fired by our MG on JUNCTION RD at Q 29 a.00.80.	
	7/11/17		Sections in the line relieved by those at ANNEQUIN. Enemy T.M. very active, several fell near KINGS RD between 11 pm and midnight. Our artillery active as usual night and day. Usual night. Harassing fire carried out by our M.G. 7000 rounds fired.	

WAR DIARY
or
INTELLIGENCE SUMMARY.
(Erase heading not required.)

Army Form C. 2118.

Place	Date	Hour	Summary of Events and Information	Remarks and references to Appendices
	8/11/17		Enemy aircraft active during the afternoon. Weather - wind and rain. Situation normal, except for our artillery which was active between 11 a.m. and 1 p.m. - Our aircraft unusually active during the morning: – Working party of 20 men elsewhere were repairs carried out. Weather fair.	
	9/11/17		Usual intelligence reports received 8 a.m. Situation quiet during the day. During the night enemy artillery much more active. Our machine guns carried out usual night harassing fire. 5000 rounds fired. Weather wind and rain.	
	10/11/17		Situation normal, except for slight activity of enemy artillery during the afternoon. Our M.G.s engaged the usual targets during the night. 5000 rounds fired. — 5000 rounds were fired by the Battery in response to an S.O.S. signal at 6.15 p.m. Working party normal. Weather wind and rain.	APPENDIX 2
	11/11/17		Situation normal. Relief was carried out by the 74th M.G. Coy. Relief was complete by 8 p.m. Weather fair.	

WAR DIARY
or
INTELLIGENCE SUMMARY.
(Erase heading not required.)

Army Form C. 2118.

Place	Date	Hour	Summary of Events and Information	Remarks and references to Appendices
	12/11/17		Preparation for smokes. Hdq and Nos. 2 & 3 sectn moved off to LE PLANTIN at 2 pm. Relf of 1/5 K.R.Coy was commenced at 4 pm. Relf was complete by 6.45 pm. Weather fair.	APPENDIX 3
	13/11/17		Situation normal, except for slight activity of enemy artillery on SHETLAND ROAD snk H.4.2¹ and H.E. dugout during the afternoon. Our Machine Guns carried out usual night Harassing fire, 7,500 rounds fired. Usual repairs carried out at NEW CUT and KING ROAD. Weather fair.	
	14/11/17		Aviation quiet. Slight activity on part of enemy aircraft. Usual targets engaged by our M.G. during the night, 7000 rounds fired. Weather fair.	
	15/11/17		Situation normal, with the exception of our artillery which was fairly active during the early part of the afternoon. Slight activity on the part of enemy machine guns, which traversed our parapet occasionally during the night. Various targets were engaged by our M. Guns	

Army Form C. 2118.

WAR DIARY
or
INTELLIGENCE SUMMARY.
(Erase heading not required.)

Instructions regarding War Diaries and Intelligence Summaries are contained in F. S. Regs., Part II. and the Staff Manual respectively. Title pages will be prepared in manuscript.

Place	Date	Hour	Summary of Events and Information	Remarks and references to Appendices
	16/11/17		6000 rounds Gun fired. Weather fair. Naval intelligence report received 8 a.m. Enemy T.M. fairly active throughout day. Hostile aeroplanes attempted to cross our line during the day. 2 were driven off by A.A. and M.G. fire. Our M.G. fired intermittently throughout the night. 8500 rounds fired. Weather sweet.	
	17/11/17		Situation normal — our artillery active all day. Enemy T.M. very active in retaliation to our artillery. Naval night harassing fire carried out by our M.G. Reinforcements J.O.R. from Rae. Weather fair.	
	18/11/17		Situation normal. Enemy artillery active in the vicinity of WINDY CORNER and GIVENCHY KEEP. Enemy T.M. fired on AVENUE & NEWCUT. Naval targets engaged by our M.Gs. Weather fair.	
	19/11/17		Situation normal. Enemy shelled GIVENCHY KEEP and MOAT FM. Enemy T.M. very active on COVIS TRENCH between 10 a.m. & noon. Bracket Artillery active between noon & 2 p.m. Photos T.M. installed.	

WAR DIARY
or
INTELLIGENCE SUMMARY.
(Erase heading not required.)

Army Form C. 2118.

Instructions regarding War Diaries and Intelligence Summaries are contained in F. S. Regs., Part II. and the Staff Manual respectively. Title pages will be prepared in manuscript.

Place	Date	Hour	Summary of Events and Information	Remarks and references to Appendices
			to enemy T.M. fire between 11.30am & 1pm. Our M.Gs fired 9000 rounds on usual targets during the night. Weather fair.	
	20/1/17		Situation normal. Our artillery fired intermittently through the day. Unusual activity of enemy aircraft during the morning. Our M.Gs engaged usual targets through the night. Weather fair.	
	21/1/17		Situation normal. Enemy working party observed about noon, but were dispersed by our M.G fire. Enemy aircraft fairly active throughout the day. Usual night firing carried out by our M.Gs 6000 rounds fired. Weather fair.	
	22/1/17		Situation normal, except for our T.M. which were unusually active during the afternoon — retaliation by enemy T.M's. Usual night harassing fire carried out. Weather overcast with rain.	
	23/1/17		Situation normal. Enemy aircraft very active all day, several crossed our lines at low altitude about 3pm. Weather cloudy.	
	24/1/17		Situation normal, aircraft between 2 & 2.45 pm when a combat round	

WAR DIARY
or
INTELLIGENCE SUMMARY.
(Erase heading not required.)

Army Form C. 2118.

Place	Date	Hour	Summary of Events and Information	Remarks and references to Appendices
			of the enemy lines in front of GIVENCHY were carried out. Our TMs cooperated in the bombardment. Enemy retaliated with shells of all calibres on GIVENCHY + also on RICHMOND TRENCH about 2.45 3 p.m. Usual day & night firing carried out by our M.Gs. Weather. Overcast. Wind and rain.	
25/11/17			Situation normal. A prisoner captured yesterday gave information to the effect that the enemy would attempt a raid on our lines with 250 men. The attack is apparently for the alteration in our dispositions to counter this. Usual night firing carried out by our Machine guns. Weather wind and rain.	APPENDIX 1
26/11/17			Situation normal. Enemy artillery shelled the vicinity of KINGS ROAD between 10am & 11am. An enemy aeroplane crossed our lines between 12.30 and 1.30 pm. Night firing carried out by our machine guns, 6500 rounds fired. Weather. Wind and rain.	

WAR DIARY or INTELLIGENCE SUMMARY.

Army Form C. 2118.

Place	Date	Hour	Summary of Events and Information	Remarks and references to Appendices
	27/11/17		Situation normal. Usual day firing by our M.G.s Weather sunà and warm	
	28/11/17		We were relieved by the 127th Machine Gun Coy. Relief was commenced at 8.30 a.m. + completed by 5.30 p.m. Coy had Breakfast at CORBIE, and finished at 9.30 a.m. and marched to HAUT RIEUX. Weather fair.	

Capt.
Commdg 7th Machine Gun Coy.

RELIEF ORDERS.   (No: 1)

1. 195.M.G.C will relieve 7.M.G.Coy on the afternoon of the 21st inst, at 4.pm.

2. O.C. No: 2 Section will hand over his 4 guns and equipment to the relieving teams, and obtain receipt for same.

3. All tripods and belt boxes will be handed over. Nos: 1, 3 and 4 Sections will only bring out guns and spare parts.

4. A guide from each team will be at Coy Hdq at 3.30.pm.

5. Guns in isolated positions will not be relieved before dusk. (i.e. after 5.pm.)

6. All emplacements and trench stores must be carefully handed over and signed receipts for trench stores handed into Coy Orderly Room by 9.am., 22nd inst.

7. Telephone instruments will be brought out.

8. T.O. will arrange for a full limber to be at ESTAMINET DUMP by 5.pm. One full limber will report at Coy Hdq at 5.30.pm.

9. On relief Sections will march to Rear Hdq at GORRE and when all Sections are present will proceed to BEUVRY.

10. A guide will meet Sections at GORRE.

11. Section Officers will report Relief Complete personally at Advanced Coy Hdq.

12. Communication trenches must be used by all teams during relief.

ACKNOWLEDGE.

20/10/17.   Commdg, 7TH MACHINE GUN COY.   Capt,

SECRET.

APPENDIX. 1.

RELEIF ORDER No 2.

1. 7th M.G.Coy. will releive 74th.M.G.Coy. on the night of 1/2nd Nov/17

2. 1 Sub-Section of No 4 Section under 2nd Lieut PEPPER will take over 4 guns in LEFT-SUB-SECTOR.

   1 Sub-section of No 3 Section under 2nd Lieut ROPER will take over 4 guns in RIGHT SUB-SECTOR.

   No 2 Section under 2nd Lieut MANNING will take over guns in BATTERY.

3. 4 guns of No4 Section will be handed over to No 2 Section. 74th M.G.Coy. will hand over 4 guns complete to No 4 Section.

4. Q.M.Stores will move to F.23.d.99. during the morning of the 1st. No 2 Section will move up to same point at 2.30.pm. Sub-sections of Nos 3 & 4 will move up at 5 pm.

5. Guides will be provided at H.Q.74th.M.G.Coy.

6. Teams will consist of 4 men per team for guns in the line.

7. Rations for 24 hours will be taken in.

8. Limbers will remain to bring out guns of 74th.M.G.Coy.

9. Orderly Room & men not detailed for trenches will move to new billets at 2.30.pm.

10. 74th M.G.Coy will hand over tripods & ammunition boxes.

11. Duplicate handing over slips will be sent up to Coy.Hdq. by 9.am. 2nd inst.

12. No 1 Section will detail 4 men to be attached to No 2 SEction. for A.A. work.

13. Situation reports willbe at Coy.Hdq. by 7.am each day..

14. Releif complete will be reported by code word DUN.

[signature] CAPT.

31/10/17.　　　　　　　　　　Commdg.7th.M.G.COMPANY.

Appendix IX
Appx 3/

Relief Order No. 3   Copy No.
            SECRET

1. 74th Machine Gun will relieve
7th Machine Gun Coy on the evening
of the 11th November 1917.

2. Personnel relieving the Battery will
arrive at HARLEY STREET about 4 pm
When relieved guns etc will be conveyed
to BEUVRY by limbers from 74th M.G.Coy.
No.1 Section on relief will proceed
direct to BEUVRY, reporting relief
complete to Coy Hdq ANNEQUIN.

(3) Personnel relieving Right and Left
Sub-Sectors will arrive about 5 pm.
74th M G Coys limbers will remain
to convey guns to BEUVRY.
On relief teams will move direct
to BEUVRY.
O.C. Sub-sectors reporting relief
complete to Coy Hdq ANNEQUIN.
All reliefs to be complete by 8 p.m.
As soon as 74th M G Coys limbers
have conveyed guns etc to BEUVRY
Sections will arrange to have them
at once unloaded and packed on
their proper limbers.
Exactly the same gun stores will
be handed over, as when the Coy
took over this Sector.

7. Billets in ANNEQUIN will be thoroughly cleaned during the morning of the 11th inst, and billet stores left in order.
There will be no working party during the morning.

8. All Coy stores not required will be loaded on two limbers which will report at Coy HdQ by 9 a.m.

9. All telephones and equipment belonging to 74th M.G. Coy, and at present in use in this Sector will be replaced by those of 74th M.G. Coy. Receipts will be obtained.

10. 7th M.G. Coy HdQ will close at ANNEQUIN at 8.30 pm and open at BEUVRY at same time.

11. 2nd Lt Ruckman will report to O.C. 74th M.G. Coy at BEUVRY during the forenoon, and take over all billets vacated by STORK.

12. All O.R at ANNEQUIN will proceed to BEUVRY at 2 pm under section Sergeants.
Signallers and HdQ will move off independently on relief.

13. Transport orders will be issued separately.

HW Ingleby Capt.
Commdg 7th M.G. Coy.

APPENDIX. No. 4

The following information was given by a German deserter who gave himself up on Right of ——— to Bde on our left.—

The 451st Inf Regt to whom he belonged were preparing for an offensive operation on the left half of our Bde front (CANADIAN ORCHARD). The strength of the attacking force was to be 250. The assault was to be proceeded by a heavy bombardment. A mine was to be exploded opposite Right of our Bde front, and followed by a front attack. The raid was to be carried out by moonlight within a few nights.

Arrangements were made as follows to counter above raid should it develop. All guns were laid on left S.O.S. targets enfilading enemy front line from which the raid was expected. Also the M.G. battery of 7-guns was laid so as to protect the ORCHARD, and an extra 4 guns borrowed from the Div. M.G. Coy was sighted so as to enfilade the same trenches these being

prepared to double barrage on
suspected area for the raid.
The raid did not develop on
either of the two remaining nights
on which this Bde was in the
line.

F.W. Jacob W.
Capt
Comndg 7th M.G. Coy

APPENDIX 3

Coy No. 5

SECRET.

RELIEF ORDERS

7TH MACHINE GUN COY will relieve 195 M.G.C. Coy during the afternoon of the 12th inst.

No. 1 SECTION.
4 guns of No 1 SECTION & 1 gun of No 3 SECTION under Lt. Rickman, will take over the 5 positions in the GIVENCHY SECTOR.

No. 2 SECTION
No. 2 SECTION with 4 guns, which will be handed over to them by No. 4 SECTION under Lt. Maddison will take over the 4 positions on the LEFT SECTOR.

No. 3 SECTION
With 3 guns under Lt. Jacob will take over the BATTERY & the 4 guns of No. 1 Section which are at present in position there.

NO. 4 SECTION.
Under 2nd Lieut Pepper will remain at GORRE.

Teams relieving Nos. 5 & 6 position will remain in the old B.L. until dusk.

GUIDES. Guides for 1, 2, & 3 Sections will be at RATION DUMP at 3.30. pm.
No. 2 Section will not move from RATION DUMP until No.1 & 3 Sections have been gone 15 minutes.

O.C. No. 3 Section will be at Battery at 2. pm.

BELTS. All belts in the line to be handed over.

RECEIPTS. Receipts for Trench Stores will be handed into Coy Hdq as soon as possible after relief.

J W Jacob Capt,
Commdg, 7TH MACHINE GUN COY.

APPENDIX 5

Secret   Copy No. 8

RELIEF ORDER No. 5.

1. 7TH M.G. Coy will be relieved by 127th M.G. Coy on the morning of the 28th inst. commencing at 4 a.m.

2. GUIDES.
   1 Guide from each team will report at Coy Hdq at 3.30 a.m.
   3 Guides will be found from Rear Hdq to conduct relieving teams to RATION CORNER.

3. TRANSPORT.
   2 limbers of 127th M.G. Coy will remain to bring out equipment from battery.
   2 limbers will be sent from the transport lines, one to be at WINDY CORNER at 5.15 a.m. to bring out equipment of RT SECTION the other to be at CROSSROADS in FESTUBERT at 5.30 a.m. to bring out equipment of LEFT SECTION.
   1 limber of 127th M.G. Coy bringing up Coy Hdq equipment at 5 a.m. will take back equipment of this Coy.
   Officers horses will be at Coy Hdq at 6 a.m.

4. All trench stores will be carefully handed over and receipts obtained.
   All belt-boxes, tripods and gun equipment will be brought out.
   Only 1 per maps will be handed over, all others will be brought out.

5. On relief teams will march to CORRE for breakfast.

6. Section Officers will report relief complete to Coy Hdq.

26-11-17.   Commdg 7TH M.G. Coy
                                                                Capt

7 M G Coy
Vol 24

WAR DIARY
or
INTELLIGENCE SUMMARY.
(Erase heading not required.)

Army Form C. 2118.

Instructions regarding War Diaries and Intelligence Summaries are contained in F. S. Regs., Part II. and the Staff Manual respectively. Title pages will be prepared in manuscript.

Place	Date	Hour	Summary of Events and Information	Remarks and references to Appendices
	29/11/17		The Coy paraded at 2.20 a.m. and marched to MAINIL there after a very strenuous march at 7.20 pm. Weather windy & cold.	
	30/11/17		The whole of the forenoon was devoted to cleaning guns & gun equipment. The C.O. made Roll & endeavoured to obtain more kilts, as the ones already allotted were insufficient to accommodate the Coy. Lt. Maddison & 2nd Lt. Piper attended a lecture on "War Aims" at COYECQUE. Weather wind & rain.	
	1/12/17		Usual parades carried out during the forenoon. Lt Madison proceeded on leave to U.K. Recreational trainings from 2 to 4 pm. Weather overcast.	
	2/12/17		Special movement order received from Bde at 1 a.m. Coy parade at 12 noon & march to CRISPY. Weather overcast. Rain overnight.	
	3/12/17		The Coy stood by during the forenoon awaiting orders which were received at 12.30 pm. Transport to move to WAVRANS at 1.30 pm. Coy parade & move to WAVRANS at 3.30 pm. The Company entrain at 6.30 pm & journey to MIRAUMONT. Weather wind & rain.	

Army Form C. 2118.

WAR DIARY
or
INTELLIGENCE SUMMARY
(Erase heading not required.)

Instructions regarding War Diaries and Intelligence Summaries are contained in F. S. Regs., Part II. and the Staff Manual respectively. Title Pages will be prepared in manuscript.

Place	Date	Hour	Summary of Events and Information	Remarks and references to Appendices
	4/12/17		Coy travelled during the night arriving at MIRAUMONT 5 p.m. After a short rest we move to COURCELLES LE COMTE, arriving there at 10.30 a.m.	
	5/12/17		Coy at rest. The remainder of the day. Weather - frosty. Coy stood by during the forenoon awaiting order for move. We paraded at 2 p.m. and march to the BARASTRE area. Weather - rain and frost.	
	6/12/17		Usual training carried out during the morning. The afternoon was devoted to recreational training. Weather - disagreeable cold.	
	7/12/17		Training as yesterday. Weather wind and rain.	
	8/12/17		Usual daily training carried out, including working of limbers. Weather. rain.	
	9/12/17		The whole of the forenoon was devoted to packing limbers and preparing for the trenches. Coy paraded at 2.45 p.m. and move into the line to relieve the 9th M.G.Coy. Relief of the 9th M.G. Coy commenced at 7.30 p.m. and was completed by 1.30 a.m. Weather. cold and rain.	APPENDIX 1

WAR DIARY or INTELLIGENCE SUMMARY.

(Erase heading not required.)

Army Form C. 2118.

Instructions regarding War Diaries and Intelligence Summaries are contained in F.S. Regs., Part II. and the Staff Manual respectively. Title pages will be prepared in manuscript.

Place	Date	Hour	Summary of Events and Information	Remarks and references to Appendices
	10/2/17		Intelligence report received 8 am. Aviation normal except for a few Enemy shell fired into LAGNICOURT about 12.15 to 1 pm. Our artillery was fairly active all day. Weather frosty.	
	11/2/17		Aviation normal – Enemy artillery active against LAGNICOURT during the morning, remainder of the day fairly quiet. Weather frosty.	
	12/2/17		Enemy artillery very active at intervals during the day on left of Bde front. – 4.2" were directed on NOREUIL NORCIES road during the forenoon. Our M.G's fired 500 rounds in response to S.O.S. signal on our left. Weather frosty.	
	13/2/17		Enemy artillery & M.G. displayed great activity on our left. Our artillery very active – bombarded Enemy trenches – Enemy positions at intervals during the day. Our aircraft very active flying at low altitude over enemy lines. Weather frosty.	
	14/2/17		Aviation normal, with the exception of our artillery which was very active between 4 + 5 pm N.E of Noreuil. Old lights in L arm were sent up from enemy line in front of the APEX	

Army Form C. 2118.

WAR DIARY
or
INTELLIGENCE SUMMARY.
(Erase heading not required.)

Instructions regarding War Diaries and Intelligence Summaries are contained in F. S. Regs., Part II. and the Staff Manual respectively. Title pages will be prepared in manuscript.

Place	Date	Hour	Summary of Events and Information	Remarks and references to Appendices
	15/12/17		Between 4 + 5 p.m. Weather frosty. Situation normal — our MG fired 1500 signals on trenches at ABBAY FARM, where considerable movement was seen during the day. Weather frosty.	
	16/2/17		Situation normal. Enemy shelled sunken road behind LEEDS RESERVE with shrapnel between 3 + 4 p.m. Weather frosty. Slight fall of snow.	
	17/2/17		Situation normal — nothing unusual to report. Weather snow-frosty.	
	18/2/17		Enemy artillery fairly active, especially between 6.30 + 7 p.m. when several shells were dropped in the vicinity of Battn Hedron H.Qrs. Our artillery active throughout the day. Our M.G. fired 2000 rounds on at road C.1.d. at irregular intervals during the night. Weather frosty.	
	19/2/17		Situation normal. 4000 rounds were fired by our MGs on track C.7.d. Weather frosty.	

Army Form C. 2118.

WAR DIARY
or
INTELLIGENCE SUMMARY.
(Erase heading not required.)

Instructions regarding War Diaries and Intelligence Summaries are contained in F.S. Regs., Part II. and the Staff Manual respectively. Title pages will be prepared in manuscript.

Place	Date	Hour	Summary of Events and Information	Remarks and references to Appendices
	20/12/17		Situation quiet. 2000 rounds fired by our M.G's at Xroads at C.I.a. Weather frosty.	
	21/12/17		Situation normal. We are relieved by the 75th M.G. Coy. Relief completed was reported by 8 p.m. Weather frosty.	APPENDIX No. 2
	22/12/17		Usual changing carried out during the forenoon. 2.45 pm Recreational training. Weather frosty.	
	23/12/17		Usual morning parade, including mechanism stoppages etc. Church parade for R.C. at 10.45 a.m. Several bombs were dropped by enemy aeroplanes in the locality of BEUGNATRE between 6 and 7 p.m. Weather frosty. Rain overnight.	
	24/12/17		Preparation made during the morning for moving for guns into the line Nos 1, 3, + Res of No 2 Section Parade for moving into the line at 2.30. p.m. Weather frosty.	APPENDIX 3.
	25/12/17		Christmas day. Recreation for Section out of the line. Weather frosty — slight fall of snow.	

WAR DIARY
or
INTELLIGENCE SUMMARY.

(Erase heading not required.)

Army Form C. 2118.

Place	Date	Hour	Summary of Events and Information	Remarks and references to Appendices
	26/12/17		Usual morning parade carried out by Sections out of the line. The two teams in the line are withdrawn at 5 pm returning to billets at 8 pm. Weather frosty — Heavy fall of snow.	APPENDIX NO 4
	27/12/17.		Owing to the majority of B Coy being in the trenches on Christmas day, to-day was devoted to recreation. Weather frosty — slight fall of snow.	
	28/12/17.		The forenoon was devoted to cleaning guns & limbers — Mechanism & stoppages. Recreational training during the afternoon. Weather frosty.	

31-12-17.

WMatthison WS
Lt Capt.
Commdg 7th M.G. Coy.

APPENDIX 1.

Relief Order No 6.   COPY NO.

Tomorrow the 7th M.G. Coy, will relieve the 9th M.G. Coy.

(2) Reveille 7 am.

(3) Blankets will be rolled, & packs put on limbers by 8.am. Jerkins and greatcoats will be kept out.

(4) Breakfast 8. am.

(5) Lt Jacobs and 2nd Lt Cooper, with one sergeant from each Section, will parade at 8 am, to reconnoitre the line.

(6) For the purpose of relief, 4 teams of 5 men each, will be arranged in each section. Three N.C.O's will accompany the sections in the line.

(7) Time of Parade will be notified later.

(8) Dress will be usual fighting order. with steel war, and jerkins greatcoats and iron-rations, and one p. of socks per man will also be carried.

(9) Details from Sections not going in the line will parade separately, under Sgt Brophy.

8/12/17

J Harrypt.
Capt.
Commdg 7th Machine Gun Coy.

APPENDIX 2

RELIEF ORDER No. 7.
by
Capt J. Best, Commdg 7th MACHINE GUN COMPANY.

1. 7th M.G.Coy will be relieved by 75th M.G.Coy on the night of the 21st/22nd.

2. Two guides from Coy Hdq will be at VAULX X roads, C.26.&.70.80 at 3.15.pm.

3. Section Officers will send a guide from each team and one for Battery to be at the Crucifix, LAGNICOURT at 4.pm.

4. Tripods and belt boxes will be handed over also all food containers.

5. All maps will be handed over and details of all work in hand and proposed.

6. One limber will report at Coy Hdq at 4.30.pm.
Two limbers will be at the CRUCFIX, LAGNICOURT, one at 5.15.pm and one at 5.45.pm.
Each limber will bring back 8 guns.

7. One man per team will remain in until dawn, when they will report to Sgt BEDDOW at present Coy Hdq and proceed with him to camp.

8. Sections on relief will march back to camp at H.10.c. independently.

9. All telephones and wires will be handed over during the morning of the 21st inst.

10. All petrol tins <u>must</u> be brought out.

11. All "handing over" receipts will be handed into the Orderly Room by 9.am. the 22nd inst.

12. Relief complete will be reported personally or by runner.

13. Horses for C.O. and Lieut Maddison will be at X roads VAULX at 7.30.pm.
Section Officers requiring their horses will notify Coy Hdq by morning intelligence.

E/C Maddison Lt
for. Capt,

20/12/17.   Commdg, 7TH MACHINE GUN COMPANY.

APPENDIX. 3.

7TH MACHINE GUN COMPANY.

OPERATION ORDERS   No. 8.

10 guns of the 7th Coy will man BATTERY positions formerly occupied by the 195 Coy.

Teams will be as follows.
(E) 2 guns of No. 2 Section under Lt. Bolam.
(D) 4 "   " No. 3 Section   "   Lt. Jacob.
(C) 4 "   " No. 1 Section   "   Lt Roper.

Teams will consist of 6 men per team.
14 belt boxes will be taken also a supply of paraffin, whale oil and water.
Further orders regarding guides etc will be issued later.

[signature]
Capt.
Commdg. 7TH MACHINE GUN COY.

APPENDIX 4

OPERATION ORDER No 9.   7TH M.G.Coy.

Ten guns of the 7th M.G.Coy will be withdrawn to-night at 5.pm.

Limbers will be at the same place as where they were unloaded at 5.pm.

Withdrawal complete will be reported to the O.C. 75th M.G.Coy who will report it to the 75th Brigade (Vide orders received from the 7th Brigade)

On withdrawal Sections will march back to Camp.

E/C Matheson Lt
for , Capt,

26/12/17.   Commdg 7th MACHINE GUN COMPANY.

7th MACHINE Gun Coy

Army Form C. 2118.

WAR DIARY
or
INTELLIGENCE SUMMARY.
(Erase heading not required.)

7 M G Coy Vol 25

Place	Date	Hour	Summary of Events and Information	Remarks and references to Appendices
	29/12/17		Usual morning parade carried out, including Barrage drill. The afternoon was devoted to Recreational Training. Weather frosty.	
	30/12/17		Morning parade as yesterday. Church parade for R.C.'s 11 a.m. Weather frosty.	
FAVREUIL	31/12/17		Men not detailed for the trenches carried out usual morning parades. Men to same detailed for the line made all preparations during the forenoon. The Lewis Gun parade at 3.30 p.m. for the line. The	APPENDIX No 1
	1/1/18		Usual morning parades carried out by men out of the line. The afternoon was devoted to Recreation. Weather frosty.	
	2/1/18		9 to 12 noon the Company prepare for moving into the trenches to relieve the 7th S.W.B. Coy. Company parade at 2.15 p.m. Relief reported complete by 6.30 p.m. Situation quiet. Weather fairly — overcast.	APPENDIX No 2
	3/1/18		Situation normal — Our artillery was fairly active shelling QUEANT at intervals. Enemy fired several shells into E end of LAGNICOURT	

Army Form C. 2118.

WAR DIARY
or
INTELLIGENCE SUMMARY.
(Erase heading not required.)

Instructions regarding War Diaries and Intelligence Summaries are contained in F. S. Regs., Part II. and the Staff Manual respectively. Title pages will be prepared in manuscript.

Place	Date	Hour	Summary of Events and Information	Remarks and references to Appendices
			about 10. a.m. and several shells dropped near Coy HQly about 11.20 p.m.	
	4/1/18		Usual night harassing fire carried out by our M.G.s 4000 round fired. Weather frosty.	
			Aviation normal. Our artillery fairly active day & night especially between 5 & 6 p.m. 6000 rounds were fired by our M.G.s on K Beat at D.I.C. 25.90. & D.7.d. 11.75. Several enemy aeroplanes attempted to cross our lines but our division Of Cys our A.A. and M.G. fire	
	5/1/18		Weather frosty. Aviation normal, with the exception of enemy artillery which shelled LAGNICOURT intermittently throughout the day. Usual night firing by our M.G.s 2000 rounds being fired. A very heavy bombardment took place on our Coy between 6.15 & 7 a.m. — Numerous Red & Green lights were sent up by the enemy. Weather frosty.	
	6/1/18		Aviation normal. Our artillery was fairly quiet all day, but recommenced in activity during the night. Usual night harassing fire carried out	

WAR DIARY
or
INTELLIGENCE SUMMARY.
(Erase heading not required.)

Army Form C. 2118.

Place	Date	Hour	Summary of Events and Information	Remarks and references to Appendices
	7/1/18		By our M.G. 3000 rounds fired. Our artillery normal all day. Increasing in activity during the night. Enemy artillery quiet. Night firing carried on by our M.G. 4000 rounds fired. Weather snow.	
	8/1/18		A very heavy bombardment took place on our left this morning between 5 & 6 am. Situation normal the remainder of the day. Weather fine.	
	9/1/18		Situation normal. Enemy artillery shelled LAGNICOURT intermittently throughout the day. Usual night firing carried out by our M.G. 3500 rounds fired. Weather rain.	
	10/1/18		Situation normal. The 75th M.G.Coy took over our Hdqs and we relieved our Hdqs of the transport Field. All details return to Transport. (F.L.O. remains at Hdqs of 75th M.G.Coy.) Weather rain - overcast.	
	11/1/18		Situation normal, with the exception of Enemy artillery which was very active all day shelling LAGNICOURT and sunken road near 75 M.G.Coy	

WAR DIARY
or
INTELLIGENCE SUMMARY.
(Erase heading not required.)

Army Form C. 2118.

Place	Date	Hour	Summary of Events and Information	Remarks and references to Appendices
	12/1/18		Hdqrs. Weather overcast - rain overnight. Situation normal. Our M.G. carried out usual night harassing fire. New Coy. Hdqrs established at C.17.a.7.3.	
	13/1/18		Weather. rain. Situation normal. Our aeroplanes were fairly active during the forenoon. Our M.G. fired 3000 rounds on road junction at D.1.d.45.60. Weather snow.	
	14/1/18		Shelling on both sides not very quiet all day, however, no activity during the night. Several shells were dropped on LAGNICOURT between 11a - 11.45 p.m. Our M.G. fired 3000 rounds. Weather snow.	
	15/1/18		Situation normal, nothing unusual to report. Weather. rain.	
	16/1/18		Situation quiet. Our M.G.s fired 3000 rounds on road junction at D.1.d.45.60. Weather. rain.	

Army Form C. 2118.

WAR DIARY
or
INTELLIGENCE SUMMARY.
(Erase heading not required.)

Instructions regarding War Diaries and Intelligence Summaries are contained in F. S. Regs., Part II. and the Staff Manual respectively. Title pages will be prepared in manuscript.

Place	Date	Hour	Summary of Events and Information	Remarks and references to Appendices
	17/1/18		Situation normal. We were relieved by the 75th Machine Gun Company. Relief was commenced at 4.30 p.m. & completed by 8 p.m. Weather rain.	APPENDIX 3
	18/1/18		General cleaning up after coming out of the line. Weather fair.	
	19/1/18		The forenoon was devoted to cleaning belts, and reposing + cleaning of limbers. Recreation the remainder of the day. Weather fair.	
	20/1/18		Church parade. A driving competition took place, between Transport drivers. Clothing was issued at 2 p.m. during the afternoon. Weather fair.	
	21/1/18		Usual morning parade carried out. C.O's inspection 11 a.m. Recreation during the afternoon. Weather fair.	

WAR DIARY
or
INTELLIGENCE SUMMARY.
(Erase heading not required.)

Army Form C. 2118.

Place	Date	Hour	Summary of Events and Information	Remarks and references to Appendices
	22/1/18		Usual morning parade carried out during the forenoon. The afternoon was devoted to recreation. Weather fair.	
	23/1/18		Parades as yesterday. Signaller Akinola to Base. Weather fair.	
	24/1/18		Usual morning parader. Workers party of Home parade at 2.45 pm for the line, returning to camp at 12.15. am 25/1/18. Bathe from 3.30 to 4.30 pm. for men in camp. Weather fair. Slight fall of rain.	
	25/1/18		The forenoon was devoted to digging protecting trenches round huts. One Sgt+one officer from each of No 3rd section parade at 7 am & proceed to reconnoitre the positions held by No. 3rd section of the 9th M.G. Coy C.O. accompanies this party. Weather fair.	
	26/1/18		During the morning section prepare for moving into the	

Army Form C. 2118.

WAR DIARY
or
INTELLIGENCE SUMMARY

(Erase heading not required.)

Instructions regarding War Diaries and Intelligence Summaries are contained in F. S. Regs., Part II. and the Staff Manual respectively. Title Pages will be prepared in manuscript.

Place	Date	Hour	Summary of Events and Information	Remarks and references to Appendices
Line	27/1/18		Relief of the 74th M.G. Coy commenced at 4.30 p.m. Relief reported complete by 7 p.m. Neard Intelligence summary received 7 a.m. Situation normal. At 7.57 p.m. Our M.G.s opened fire immediately, firing 20 rounds on S.O.S. lines. Enemy aeroplanes crossed our lines between 10 p.m. & 12 midnight. Weather fair.	APPENDIX No. 4
	28/1/18		Artillery on Btk sides was fairly active during day & night. Enemy aeroplanes displayed great activity all day. Several crossed our lines about 6 p.m. & worked back areas. Weather fair.	

31-1-18.

Alex ...... Capt.
Comdg 74 Machine Gun Coy.

APPENDIX No 1.

7TH MACHINE GUN COMPANY.

Ten guns of the 7th machine Gun Company will take over "E" "D" and "C" Batteries tonight.

Two guns of No. 2. SECTION under 2nd Lt Cooper will take over "E" Battery.

4 guns of No 4. SECTION under 2nd Lt Pepper will take over "D" Battery.

Four teams (made up from men who were not in the line last time) under 2nd Lt Manning will take over "C" Battery.

GUIDES. Guides for Batteries will be at the undermentioned places at 6pm.

"C" Battery.   X Roads near 74th Bde. Hdq.
"D" Battery.   75TH M.G. Coy Hdq.
"E" Battery.   Crucifix, Lagnicourt.

BELT BOXES.   14 belt boxes per gun will be taken into the line.

Teams will parade at 3.30.pm.

31/12/17.

Capt ███████

Commdg 7TH MACHINE GUN COY.

APPENDIX. No 2

RELIEF ORDER. No. 10.

(1) **7TH M.G.s.** will relieve **74TH M.G.C.** in the line on the night of the 2/3rd Jan/1918. passing Xroads VAULX at 4.15

(2) 2nd Lt Manning will take over Nos. 12 and 13 positions and E(1) and E(2) Battery positions
Teams of No. 2 Section at present in B Battery will take over the two Battery positions
2nd Lt Casper will see the latter relief carried out and report to 2nd Lt Manning before leaving the line.

(3) 3 guns of No. 1 section under 2nd Lt Balam will relieve guns at Nos. 9,10, and 11 positions.

(4) 4 guns of No. 4 Section with one gun of No. 1 Section under 2nd Lt Pepper will relieve guns Nos. 14,15,16,17, and 18.

(5) 4 guns of No. 3 Section under Lt Jacob will relieve "F" Battery

(6) The two teams of No. 1 Section and the two teams of No. 3 Section at present in C Battery will be at the Crucifix at 4.30.pm and meet the remainder of their Sections.

(7) Officers in charge of C and D Batteries will see that teams are reduced to 4 men per team before leaving the Battery positions, the extra men will be sent to Coy. Hdq. and will march down to camp under 2nd Lt Casper.

(8) Tripods and ammunition of 8 guns in D and E Battery positions will be collected at Crucifix Corner by 4.30 pm and will go down on returning limbers of **7TH M.G.C.** Coy.
O.C. **75TH M.G.C.** will arrange to remove tripods and ammunition from C Battery.

(9) GUIDES. as under will be at Crucifix Corner at 4.40pm.

    2 guides for 5 guns 14 to 18.
    1 guide for F Battery.
    1 guide for 2 guns 12 and 13.
    1 guide for 3 guns 9 to 11.

(10) LIMBERS. 1 limber for No. 1 Section, and No. 3 Section
    1 half limber for No. 4 Section.
    1 limber for Headquarters.

(11) Signallers will proceed up the line on the morning of the 2nd inst. and take over all phones and wires

(12) All maps and details of work in hand will be taken over Duplicate lists of trench stores will be sent to Coy. Hdq. with the Intelligence Summary at 7.30am on the morning of the 3rd inst.

(13) Rations for the line will be sent to Crucifix Corner each night at 5.30 pm

(14) Relief complete will be reported to Coy. Hdq. by code word NOTE.

                        Capt.

            Commdg 7TH MACHINE GUN COMPANY.

SECRET   APPENDIX No 3
RELIEF ORDER No 77   Coy No.

75TH M.G.Coy   7TH M.G.C.

1. ~~75th~~ will relieve ~~7th~~ on the night of the 17/18th Jany/18.
2. All positions at present occupied by ~~7th~~ 7HMGC will be taken over.
3. **GUIDES** No guides will be required for old positions. O.C. No 3 Section will detail one guide for new Battery position, to be at his Section Hdq.
4. **RELIEF** The relief of 12 guns will be carried out at dusk. 4 guns (as yet unknown) will be relieved later owing to inter-company relief between the other two companies in the line.
   These four guns will be reported to the Officer concerned when known.
5. **LIMBERS** One limber will be at Crucifix at 6 p.m. and will take the first 12 guns.
   The remaining four guns will be carried out. Hdq. One limber will report at Coy Hdq at 5 p.m.
6. All tripods, belt-boxes, gun tools, maps, trenches stores, and details of work in hand will be handed over.
7. On relief sections will march back to No 5 Camp (previous rest camp).
8. Relief complete will be reported personally or by runner to Coy Hdq.

17-1-18   J. Best Capt
                 Commdg ~~75th~~ 7TH M.G.Coy

APPENDIX No 4

SECRET   **RELIEF ORDERS.**   COPY No.

(1) The 7TH MACHINE GUN COMPANY will relieve the 74TH MACHINE GUN COY. on the night of the 26/27/JAN/1918. relief complete to be complete by midnight 26th inst.

(2) No 1 SECTION will relieve "A" Battery.
No 2 SECTION will relieve Nos 1,2,3 & 4 positions.
No 3 SECTION will relieve "B" Battery.
No 4 SECTION will man "B2" Battery.

Guides.
SECTIONS and transport will move up independently.
One mounted guide per limber will be picked up at transport lines 74TH MACHINE GUN COMPANY. (WACKLAND LINES) at 4pm.
One guide per SECTION will meet SECTIONS at H.Q. 74TH Bde Hdq at 4.30 pm.and guide them to SECTION Hdq. where limbers will be met and guides for each team provided where necessary.
One guide for Hdq will also be at Hdq. 74TH Bde.

(4) Nos 1,2,& 3 SECTIONS will take over tripods and belt boxes of 74TH MACHINE GUN COMPANY. No 4 SECTION will take in 16 belt boxes per gun

(5) 74TH MACHINE GUN COMPANY will leave a No 1 at each gun position untill 5.30 pm 27th inst.

(6) Water tins will be taken in, Water to be drawn by SECTIONS from tanks provided in the line.

(7) Rations will be brought up each night to SECTION Hdq.
One half limber will be datailed for Hdq.

(8) Telephones will be taken over by day on the 26th inst.

(9) Intelligence will be sent to Coy. Hdq. by 6.30.am each morning.

(10) Maps,trench stores,and all details of work,in hand will be taken over ,. Duplicate receipts will be sent to Hdq.

(11) Relief complete will be reported to Coy. Hdq. by code phrase "G.M. received - Pm.

(12) Teams for 1,2,& 3 positions will consist of 4 men per team Battery teams will be 6 men per team.

(13) Lt.J.M.Laing will remain in No 5 Camp in charge of details.

                         Capt.
              Commdg 7TH MACHINE GUN COMPANY.

77th MACHINE GUN COMPANY

WAR DIARY or INTELLIGENCE SUMMARY.

Army Form C. 2118.

(Erase heading not required.)

Place	Date	Hour	Summary of Events and Information	Remarks and references to Appendices
	29/1/18		Situation normal. Enemy shells Lagnicourt, Pronville Valley and rear areas, at intervals during day & night. Our M.Gs fire occasional bursts. Kicking for several enemy aeroplanes cross our lines between 9 and 10 p.m. a tank back area. Weather fair.	
	30/1/18		Situation normal, with the exception of enemy artillery what continued shelling Lagnicourt, Pronville Valley. Aircraft on both sides fairly active all day. Several enemy planes attempted to cross our lines, but are prevented from doing so by our A.A. guns. Weather fair.	
	31/1/18		Situation normal. Intermittent shelling by enemy artillery of Roads & Valley in D.19.C. during the night. (calibre 4.2" and 5.9".) Occasional bursts were fired by enemy M.Gs, but on no special target. Weather misty.	
	1/2/18		Situation normal. Enemy shelled Road & Valley in D.19.C. during the early part of the night, otherwise nothing unusual to report. Weather misty. Frost.	
	2/2/18		Our artillery was fairly active all day, especially on right Divisional front. Enemy shells Road & Valley in D.19.C. & several shells were	J.W.

Army Form C. 2118.

WAR DIARY
or
INTELLIGENCE SUMMARY.
(Erase heading not required.)

Instructions regarding War Diaries and Intelligence Summaries are contained in F. S. Regs., Part II. and the Staff Manual respectively. Title pages will be prepared in manuscript.

Place	Date	Hour	Summary of Events and Information	Remarks and references to Appendices
	3/2/18		Fired in J.16 about 12 noon. (calibre 4.2"). Aircraft on both sides fairly active all day, & again during the night when enemy bombed back area. Weather bright & clear. Artillery on both sides fairly active all day. Enemy shells Road & Valley in D.19.C. between 9 a.m. & 10 a.m. Hostile parties were seen in the vicinity of PRONVILLE, and were dispersed by our M.G. fire. Between 6. + 6.30 p.m. intermittent bursts were fired on sunken road in D. 21. B. ALLEMAND gun fired on HINDENBURG Front line between 6.20 & 9.30 p.m. This was done at the request of O.C. Fright Battalion to assist a fighting patrol. Considerable aerial activity on both sides all day. Enemy observation balloon sent al great height. Weather mild, clear.	
	4/2/18		Enemy artillery fairly active all day shelled J.2.9. continuously with shell of large calibre between 7.30 & 9.30 p.m. Shrapnel barrage put down by our artillery in D.21.L. between 7 + 8 p.m. Aerial Pirates (aeroplanes) reported dispersed by our M.G. in vicinity of PRONVILLE. 3200 rounds fired by our M.G. on S.O.S. lines. Two other guns (ADAM and APPLE) fired occasional bursts in vicinity of NIXTAL~ D.21.a.29.	[signature]

(A7092.) Wt. W12859/M1293. 750,000. 1/17. D.D. & L., Ltd. Forms/C.2118/14.

WAR DIARY or INTELLIGENCE SUMMARY

Army Form C. 2118.

Place	Date	Hour	Summary of Events and Information	Remarks and references to Appendices
	5/2/18		No accidt: operation of Inf patrol. Weather dry - overcast. Enemy heavily bombard our front and support line between 4-6 a.m. Active again between 11.1 pm + 12 midnight in vicinity of Road + Valley D.19.c. + D.25.a. Our artillery continuously active during the day + early part of the night. Several attempts made by enemy aircraft to cross our lines, but are driven back by our aeroplanes and A.A. fire. Weather Bright + clear.	
	6/2/18		Situation normal, with the exception of our artillery which shelled enemy defences S.W. of PRONVILLE at intervals during day + night. Two of our forward M.G. in LEECH AVENUE carried out harassing fire between 8pm + 4.30.a.m. (1.2.18) Targets - X Roads D.9.d. 45.20. MELBOURNE 17 from D.10.c.2510 to D.10.c.43.33. Weather Fair	
	7/2/18		Situation normal. Valley near T.2. dump shelled by enemy in the evening, otherwise nothing unusual to report. Weather overcast - slight fall of rain.	

Army Form C. 2118.

WAR DIARY
or
INTELLIGENCE SUMMARY.
(Erase heading not required.)

Instructions regarding War Diaries and Intelligence Summaries are contained in F. S. Regs., Part II. and the Staff Manual respectively. Title pages will be prepared in manuscript.

Place	Date	Hour	Summary of Events and Information	Remarks and references to Appendices
	8/9/18		Situation normal. Nothing unusual to report. Shelled LAGNICOURT between 6+10 p.m. Weather fair.	
	9/9/18		Situation normal, with the exception of a heavy bombardment which took place on our left between 5.20 - 6.30 a.m. LAGNICOURT shelled at intervals throughout the day. Weather fair - slight fall of rain.	
	10/9/18		Situation normal. We are relieved by the 121st Machine Gun Coy. Relief commenced at 5 p.m. + complete by 9.30 p.m. Weather cold + damp.	APPENDIX 1.
	11/9/18		The forenoon was devoted to packing limbers and preparing for move to new area. Company parade at 2 p.m. and march to ACHIET area. Weather fair.	
	12/9/18		The forenoon was devoted to entrenching kits against enemy aircraft. Remainder of the day. Renaudin the Pte (now Corpl) Everett awarded the BELGIUM CROIX DE GUERRE. Weather fair.	

WAR DIARY
or
INTELLIGENCE SUMMARY.
(Erase heading not required.)

Army Form C. 2118.

Place	Date	Hour	Summary of Events and Information	Remarks and references to Appendices
	13/9/18		Entrenching tuts against enemy aircraft. Baths are allotted to the Company at MEHIET LE PETIT. between 10.a.m and 12.noon. War Savings Certificates sold to the value of £287-6-0. Weather. Fair.	
	14/9/18		Work of entrenching tuts against enemy aircraft continued during the forenoon. Recreation the remainder of the day. Weather. Fair.	
	15/9/18		The morning was devoted to continuation of work on tuts. 2 to 3 pm Cleaning up. 3 to 4 pm Kit inspection. Weather Fair.	
	16/9/18		Work on tuts as yesterday during the forenoon. The afternoon was devoted to cleaning of all equipment, firearms etc. Weather Fair.	
	17/9/18		Voluntary RCs & Nonconformist service at MEHIET LE GRAND. Men not attending church service continued work on tuts. Inter-Company football match played during the afternoon 7th M.G.Coy. v 74th M.G.Coy. Weather fine.	

WAR DIARY or INTELLIGENCE SUMMARY

Army Form C. 2118.

(Erase heading not required)

Instructions regarding War Diaries and Intelligence Summaries are contained in F.S. Regs., Part II. and the Staff Manual respectively. Title pages will be prepared in manuscript.

Place	Date	Hour	Summary of Events and Information	Remarks and references to Appendices
	18/2/18	8.45 to 9.45 a.m	Company parade for drill under the adjutant. Usual parades carried out during the remainder of the morning. Signallers parade at 10. a.m under the Battalion Signalling Officer. 2 to 4 pm Gun Drill. Weather frosty.	
	19/2/18		Usual morning parades carried out. All attached men not selected for transfer parade at 10. a.m in rear of Batt O/Rooms to continue work on Rifle Gun Drill during the afternoon. Weather fair.	
	20/2/16		Section parade at 60 minute intervals commencing 8.45 to 9.45 Drill. Weather fair. 2 to 4 pm Gun Drill.	
	21/2/18	10 am for Baths.	During the morning usual parades were carried out. At 4 pm the Coys (including transport) paraded for Gas Inspection and test, at Divisional Gas School. Weather fair. Slight fall of snow.	
	22/2/18		Parades as yesterday during the forenoon. All attached men for those selected for transfer paraded at 2.30. pm and return to their respective Battalions. Recreation during the afternoon. Weather fair.	

J.W.

Army Form C. 2118.

WAR DIARY
or
INTELLIGENCE SUMMARY.
(Erase heading not required.)

Instructions regarding War Diaries and Intelligence Summaries are contained in F. S. Regs., Part II. and the Staff Manual respectively. Title pages will be prepared in manuscript.

Place	Date	Hour	Summary of Events and Information	Remarks and references to Appendices
	23/2/18		8.45 to 11 am. was devoted to cleaning all equipment, tent etc. At 11.15. am. the Coy commander inspected the Coy. DREW. fighting order. 12 to 12.30. pm 73rd Reformation Drill. An inter-company football match took place during the afternoon 7 M.M.G.Coy. v. 75th M.G.Coy. Weather fair.	
	24/2/18		Church Parade during the morning. Battalion sports were held on the football ground, commencing at 1.30. pm. Weather fair. slight fall of rain.	
	25/2/18		Usual morning parades during the forenoon. Lecture to all officers of the Company from 2 to 3. pm. Weather fair.	
	26/2/18		8.45 to 9.45 Usual morning drill parade. 10 to 12 noon Limber Drill. 12 to 12.30 pm. Physical Training. Lecture for all officers from 2 to 3 pm. Weather fair.	Nil

Army Form C. 2118.

WAR DIARY
or
INTELLIGENCE SUMMARY.
(Erase heading not required.)

Instructions regarding War Diaries and Intelligence Summaries are contained in F. S. Regs., Part II. and the Staff Manual respectively. Title pages will be prepared in manuscript.

Place	Date	Hour	Summary of Events and Information	Remarks and references to Appendices
	27/2/18		Parades as yesterday during the forenoon. The afternoon was devoted to cleaning all equipment etc. pending inspection by the Corps Commander. Weather rain.	
	28/2/18		Company on the range from 9am until 1pm.	

J H Ewing, Lieut.
for Capt.
Commdg 7 K Mackur Gun Company

APPENDIX No 1

SECRET.   RELIEF ORDER NO. 12.   COPY NO.

(1) 7TH MACHINE GUN COMPANY will be relieved by the 18TH MACHINE GUN COY. on the night of the 10/11th February /1918.

(2) GUIDES.
        1 guide from Nos 1 & 2 positions.
        1 " " " 3 & 4 positions.
        1 " " each Battery A.B.B2.
will meet incoming Company at sunken road MORCHIES. I.6.c.6.0. at 5.pm.

(3) Tripods and belt boxes will be taken out. Arrangements may be made in regard to exchanging 14 belt boxes. per gun. Notification of this will be made later.

(4) TRENCH STORES.
        All trench stores will be carefully handed over and receipts obtained.

(5) MAPS.
        All maps 1/20,000 and 1/10,000 of this area will be handed over.

(6) TRANSPORT.
        Limbers of incoming Coy will take out guns etc of this Company.
One limber of 7TH MACHINE GUN COMPANY will report at Coy Hdq. at 6.pm.

(7) On relief Company will march to No 5 Camp FAVREUIL.

(8) Transport OFFICER 7TH MACHINE GUN COY. will arrange to hand over his transport lines to 18TH MACHINE GUN COMPANY, on the 10th inst. His transport will be picketed for the night in the field adjoining No 5 Camp.

(9) Completion of relief will be reported to Coy Hdq by 'phone or runner, by code phrase M.G.12 received -- Pm.

                                                        Capt.
            Commdg 7TH MACHINE GUN COMPANY.

www.ingramcontent.com/pod-product-compliance
Lightning Source LLC
Chambersburg PA
CBHW081527160426
43191CB00011B/1700